TARA BROWNER

Heartbeat of the People

Music and Dance of the Northern Pow-wow

UNIVERSITY OF ILLINOIS PRESS

URBANA AND CHICAGO

First paperback edition, 2004
© 2002 by the Board of Trustees
of the University of Illinois
All rights reserved
Manufactured in the United States of America
1 2 3 4 5 C P 5 4 3 2 1

⊗ This book is printed on acid-free paper.

The Library of Congress cataloged the hardcover edition
as follows:
Browner, Tara, 1960–
Heartbeat of the people : music and dance of the
northern pow-wow / Tara Browner.
p. cm. — (Music in American life)
Includes bibliographical references (p.) and index.
ISBN 0-252-02714-0 (cloth)
1. Powwows—North America—History.
2. Indian dance—North America.
3. Indians of North America—Songs and music.
I. Title. II. Series.
E98.P86B76   2002
781.62'97—dc21   2001003564

Paperback ISBN 0-252-07186-7

HEARTBEAT OF THE PEOPLE

MUSIC IN AMERICAN LIFE

A list of books in the series appears at the end of this book.

To Cloyd Duff,

friend, my friend

Contents

Acknowledgments

I could not have completed the manuscript for this book without the help and encouragement of friends, family, and colleagues. First, I would like to say *pilamaya* to Norma, Robert, Chanda, and Aspen Rendon, January Little, and Nadine and Ardie Janis, Jr., and *miigwetch* to George, Sydney, and Shannon Martin and David and Punkin Shananaquet. Without their words, this book would have been much poorer. Many thanks are also due to my pow-wow "family," including Sue Hill (who did the machine sewing on my first Jingle Dance outfit), Stephanie Fitzgerald (she also sews), Ruth Bayhylle for her insights about Southern Great Plains pow-wow musical styles, and Dorene and Shawna Red Cloud.

Thanks also to those who read portions of the manuscript: Richard Haefer, Sam Cronk, Tim Rice, Mitchell Morris, and Helen Rees. All assisted at one point or another in jump-starting my brain (yes, it did die a few times). Others who helped at different stages include my good friend Crisca Bierwert, Ed Wapp (of the American Indian Institute of the Arts), Irving "Hap" McCue, Bob Red Elk, Ronnie Theisz, Inés Hernádez-Avila, Kerwin George, and Hanay Geiogamah.

At various times I received technical assistance from the following individuals: the Red Cloud sisters (again), Jessica Waldemar, Gee Rabe, Andrew Connell, Omid Bürgen, Glenn Pillsbury, and Roselle Kipp. All of it was very much appreciated, especially since my finale skills still languish at a 1993 level of competence. Thanks also to the staff of the UCLA ethnomusicology department, including Donna Armstrong, Shána Garrett, Carole Pratt, Valerie Rose, Diane Roberts, Betty Price, Tom Withey, and the ever-helpful Louise Spear of the UCLA Ethnomusicology Archive.

Special thanks to the folks at the University of Illinois Press, including Judith McCulloh, Margo Cheney, Terry Sears, Copenhaver Cumpston, Mary Giles, and readers A, B, and C. In addition, I was treated wonderfully by the library and archive staff of the Buffalo Bill Historical Center in Cody, Wyoming, and recommend the center to anyone who is traveling through northern Wyoming and has a day to spare looking at cool stuff.

In various stages of this project I received financial assistance from the Ford Foundation, the University of California, Los Angeles Institute of American Cultures (IAC), the UCLA Academic Senate Grants Program, and—early on—from the Foundation of the University of Wisconsin College, West Bend, where I taught briefly before joining the faculty at UCLA.

Finally, special thanks to those along the way who gave me encouragement, including Richard Crawford, Margaret Hamilton, Glenn Watkins, Cloyd Duff (my *mafo*, timpani teacher, and friend of many years), and my mother, Leota Axford Browner, whose love of music was the root of my own. And, even though he has been gone for many years, I also acknowledge my grandfather, Cecil Monroe (Wesley) Browner, who, when he said "never forget your Indian blood," sent me on a journey that is not yet over.

Notes on Terminology
and Capitalization

Writing about pow-wows and the Indians who live them is a venture having its own set of political issues, many of which hinge upon word choices. The most immediate is how to refer to the people I discuss. After giving the matter some thought, I decided to use a variety of terms, including *Indian, American Indian, Native American, Native Canadian, Native North American, First Nations,* and *indigenous,* because all are used by Native American Indians when writing about themselves. Choosing only one would make for monotonous reading; in addition, I have seen every one of these terms in either Indian newspapers or literature produced by the tribes (some of whom refer to themselves as "tribes," whereas others call themselves "nations"). I will use the words *tribe, nation,* and *people* interchangeably because no one term is universally embraced by all Native people in everyday conversation.

Creative use of capitalization is a policy to which I also subscribe, for the most part because I try as much as possible to retain Native word usage in regard to music and dance terminology. At pow-wows, both the drum used for performance and those who play it while singing are referred to metonymically as a "drum." For the purposes of this text, I shall use the word *Drum* in reference to Drum groups and *drum* when referring to instruments, a practice now standard among most scholars who write about pow-wows. Also, I will capitalize the word *Dance* when it refers to a specific event or pow-wow and use lower-case to invoke the physical act of dancing or a particular style of dancing. Finally, I will capitalize the word *pow-wow* when referring to a specific event (for example, the Ann Arbor, Michigan, Pow-wow) and use lower-case when discussing pow-wows in general.

HEARTBEAT OF THE PEOPLE

1 *All about Theory, Method, and Pow-wows*

Just what is a pow-wow? When teaching courses on Native American music, I always start the unit on intertribal pow-wows by having the students memorize the following phrase: "A pow-wow is an event where American Indians of all nations come together to celebrate their culture through the medium of music and dance." In every mid-term examination that same definition echoes back at me in scores of essays. An annual on-campus pow-wow provides an easy field trip for my class, complete with live music, dance, high-calorie food, and shopping opportunities. As an added bonus, students can take photographs, purchase recordings, and talk to dancers, musicians, vendors, and other spectators.

I begin my classroom discussion of pow-wow music with a general history—including traditional, pre-pow-wow forms of dance—and move through the topics of regalia and dance styles, musical expression, an outdoor lesson on intertribal dancing (yes, I make students dance), and a lesson on protocols and dance arena lay-out. Students are then required to attend a pow-wow (usually the UCLA spring event) and while there to talk to musicians and dancers in a (hopefully) unintrusive manner. When it became time to write a book on the subject, I finally settled, after months of worrying about how to present my research in narrative form, on a chapter order that exactly mirrored the order of my teaching. Because my instructional style has been honed by reading scores of papers and essay examinations, following the syllabus seemed a sensible enough approach to writing a book-length manuscript.

Intertribal pow-wows are the most widespread venues for traditional Indian music and dance in North America. They are held each weekend within a reasonable driving distance (approximately three hours) of every populated area in the United States and Canada. The events can draw dancers and Drum groups from hundreds of miles away, as well as numerous Indian and non-Indian traders and spectators. For many urban Native families, they provide a community gathering place where friends and relatives come together on weekends for those rare occasions when other Indians constitute a majority and are able to interact in a culturally safe space.

Some scholars, such as Weibel-Orlando (1991), have characterized pow-wows as inauthentic renditions of a glorified past, simulations without internal cultural referents, and elaborate ethnic theaters where Indians construct an idealized identity and present it to outsiders. In "Pan-Indianism in Native American Music and Dance," James Howard sums up that attitude with the phrase "better Pan-Indian than no Indian" (1989:80). Although admittedly pow-wows do contain elements of theater—especially the competitive events—they are far more complex musically and socially than Howard is willing to concede. For whatever reasons, he and many other writers before 1990 insisted that in order for any Indian event to be musically and kinesthetically "authentic," participants had to embrace an aesthetic similar to that found in the rendezvous encampments of the American Mountain Man Society. In that group, no article of clothing or weapon can be displayed that came into use as a trade good after 1840.[1] Pow-wow participants, however, are not like Civil War reenactors. Although they dance and sing in ways drawn from historical tradition, they do so in the present—and to serve contemporary purposes and needs.

Yet in the late twentieth and early twenty-first centuries, when so many things Indian have been commodified, pow-wows remain contradictory, challenging both observers and participants to find meaning within a pastiche of tradition and commercialism. Continually changing musical repertories, dance styles, and regalia combine with new traditions to create an ongoing state of transformation that often coexists uneasily with the older Native mores that demand adherence to custom in dress, behavior, and music. Yet underneath the layers of representation is a living event, central to the lives of participants who may travel hundreds of miles each week for the chance to "dress to dance" or sing for the money collected during a Blanket Dance.

An Overview

Within the larger pow-wow circuit there are two basic types of event: "Northern" and "Southern." The Northern style began in the Northern Great Plains and the Great Lakes regions and now occurs throughout the northern tier of states and in Canada. Southern pow-wows sprang from unique circumstances in Oklahoma, where numbers of unrelated tribes were crowded together during the mid- to late nineteenth century and where the concepts of "pan-Indianism" or "intertribalism" were born from necessity. For the most part, the dividing line between Southern and Northern events is geographic. Everything south of the Oklahoma-Kansas border is Southern. Events held north of that line, including the mid- and Northern Great Plains, Pacific Northwest, Great Lakes region, and all of Canada, are considered Northern.[2] There are a few exceptions, notably with the Southern singing style of the Wisconsin Ho-Chunk (Winnebago) existing in immediate proximity to the Northern style of Ojibwe and Menominee people. Even though Ho-Chunk singing is Southern in character, they consider their pow-wows Northern, which makes singing style not entirely indicative of overall pow-wow conceptual framework. In addition, in some areas, such as southern California, events often combine Northern and Southern traditions, although, in my experience, a Southern sensibility seems to predominate.

My examination of the Northern-style pow-wow uses two indigenous metaphors: the Sacred Hoop and the Sacred Fire. The former is from the Lakota people (including the Nakota and Dakota), and the latter from the Anishnaabeg Three Fires Confederacy (Ojibwe, Odawa, and Bodewaadmi). For the Lakota, the Sacred Hoop symbolizes a protective spiritual force that surrounds them. The Anishnaabeg Sacred Fire serves as a central focal point, bringing together the "Three Fires"—the three nations making up the Anishnaabeg Confederacy. Unfolding in the spatial arrangement of pow-wow dance arenas, these metaphors inform song texts and dance styles as well.

The Lakota and the Anishnaabeg have two distinctive gathering traditions, those of the *wacipi* (the Lakota term for a dance event) and "camp meetings" (Anishnaabeg), a term describing Christian revivals that was appropriated by the Great Lakes Indians to also represent ceremonial gatherings and dances. Informing underlying concepts of what a pow-wow is, regional conventions also create larger meanings within the greater, pan-Indian pow-wow culture and the dominant society. Diversity of regalia, dance footwork, order of events, protocols, and—to a lesser extent—singing styles can be traced to pre-pow-wow gatherings before the onset of intertribal assemblies. Many fundamental differences between the Great Plains and Great Lakes regions persisted in the late twentieth century despite the fact that pow-wows in both regions share common forms of music and dance and many of the same musicians and dancers.

Many scholars have focused on the pan-Indian elements present at pow-wows and posited a loss of individual tribal identity in favor of a kind of culturally homogenized "super-Indian." My thesis is the opposite— that *all* pow-wows have a larger, underlying tribal or regional framework, and by either merging with or deviating from it participants reenforce personal tribal affiliations. In other words, Lakota dancers who attend Rosebud Fair are in for an empowering, Lakota-centric cultural experience. The same persons, when visiting Pawnee Fair, would still feel welcome and enjoy the overall atmosphere but would not feel pride in being Pawnee. They would feel "different" and in that contrast would be reminded of their Lakota identity. That is not to suggest that Indians define themselves as individuals by dissimilarities, because they do not. But in a larger, group-oriented sense, tribal people share common languages, histories, customs, and blood with others of their tribe. The ties that bind them also set them apart from those not of their nation. I am not implying the nonexistence of a larger, overarching "Indian" identity or that "Indian-ness" as a concept is not celebrated at pow-wows. For most Native people, however, even those who live in urban areas, tribal identity comes first, Indian identity second, and national identity (American or Canadian) third.

Ethnology, Theory, and Native Musical Expression

Native North Americans are one of the most ethnographically documented groups in the world. Most early American ethnological texts were built on studies of Indian cultures, and that body of earlier work— from approximately 1850 through the 1920s—profoundly informs and influences contemporary scholarship. It is impossible to escape this legacy. Fieldwork conducted by such luminaries as Frances Densmore, Alice Fletcher, and James Mooney is the basis for much of what modern scholars—and many Indians as well—know about the musical practices of more than a century ago. No matter what the theoretical and racial biases of these researchers, their field recordings constitute a legacy that survived almost fifty years of government-sponsored suppression of traditional culture and religion. Their writings, although often useful, constitute a mixed inheritance, part factual blessing and part theoretical curse.

The science of ethnology—now subsumed by the larger discipline of anthropology—had its roots in the United States, with government and academically sponsored studies (many of which focused on music and dance) of indigenous people. The first doctoral dissertation in the field of "comparative-musicology" was Theodore Baker's "Über die Musik der nordamerikanischen Wilden" (On the music of the North American Indians), completed in 1882 for the University of Leipzig. Ethnologist Jesse Walter Fewkes's inaugural field recordings of music at Zuni Pueblo in 1889 constituted another first in the study of American Indian cultures.

The value of their research notwithstanding, most early ethnologists who studied Native cultures were government employees, not academics. With a few notable exceptions, for example, the cultural relativist Franz Boas, ethnology as a whole supported a social Darwinist agenda that justified Manifest Destiny and the relegation of Indians to reservations until such time as they were judged fit to join dominant society. Indian music was collected out of an intellectual curiosity often unconnected with any sense of aesthetic appeal.

By the 1890s the concentration of Native people onto small, confined areas of reservation land was national policy, giving ethnologists rare access to Indian cultures. Armed with the new Edison cylinder and Berliner disc recording technologies, they visited reservations, eager to record songs of "vanishing" Americans before the Bureau of Indian Affairs (at that time part of the War Department) could outlaw the songs' performance in ceremonial context. Motivations varied from a genuine desire to document and possibly save musical traditions thought to be on the wane (now popularly known as "salvage ethnomusicology") to a form of what anthropologist Renato Rosaldo (1989) has termed "imperialistic nostalgia"—a melancholy longing by a people or culture for what they have destroyed. In the meantime, the Bureau of Indian Affairs had free reign in its attempts to begin the assimilation of Native populations. The stated goal, according to the 1887 Dawes Act, was "breaking up the tribal mass" and alloting reservation lands to individual tribespeople, with surplus lands made available to homesteaders.

By the early 1890s, ethnologists such as Alice Fletcher had begun systematic, large-scale studies of regional Native American musical repertories. Fletcher, in tandem with her adopted son Francis LaFlesche (Omaha), published *A Study of Omaha Indian Music* (1893), one of the earliest, most complete studies of a Native musical repertory based upon systematic research and fieldwork. Inspired by Fletcher's undertaking, Frances Densmore traveled to a number of Minnesota Ojibwe (Chippewa) settlements to learn about and document their music. In 1910 she produced the first of what would be more than a dozen works on Native music and culture: *Chippewa Music* (volume 1). Densmore still ranks as the most prolific writer on Indian music. She made hundreds of field recordings—spanning almost half a century—that constitute a valuable resource for ethnomusicologists as well as the larger Indian community.

Most early research on American Indian music was informed by a set of theories of cultural evolution popular from about 1850 through 1920. Seen in this context, aboriginal people around the globe existed in the present as representatives of the European past. Moreover, Native American melodies were universal rather than specific to Indian people, because all human cultures had moved through the uniform theoretical model first developed by ethnologist Lewis Henry Morgan, which he termed "cultural evolutionary stages" (CES).[3] At a time when human musical expression was classified according to whether it was "primitive" or "civilized," most ethnologists assumed that Native American music— because it was performed predominantly by human voices with percussion accompaniment—must be primitive. Following that logic, Indian music would sound similar to that of early Europeans, making Indians a living laboratory for learning about European prehistory. As Mary Tivey, an anthropologist, has observed (1993:9), museum exhibits of the time were dominated by the presentation style: "From the 1870s through the 1890s a comparative model placed Indians and their objects low on an evolutionary tree divided into several linear stages of cultural and biological human evolution, extending from savagery through barbarism and civilization. Because this uniform model implied that Indians lived an earlier form of life once experienced by Europeans, Native artifacts were believed to provide an historical understanding of the early stages of the evolution of Western Culture."

Alice Fletcher's belief in the theory of "cultural evolutionary stages" is apparent in her writing. In the introductory chapters of *Indian Story and Song from North America*, a collection of oral texts and songs in harmonized settings, she notes:

> Scholars are recognizing that the aboriginal conditions on this continent throw light on the slow development of human society and its institutions. . . . As these songs are from a race practically without instruments,—for the drum and rattle were only used to accentuate rythm [*sic*],—they are representative of the period when the human voice was the sole means of musical expression,—a period which antedated the invention of instruments by an immeasurable time. . . . The art of poetry is here in its infancy, giving even less sign of its future development than music, which had already acquired the outline of that form which

has since crystallised into the art of music. . . . Like the swelling buds on the bare branch, which hint the approach of summer's wealth, so these little vocables and rythmic [*sic*] devices whisper the coming of the poets. (1900:120, 124, 126)

Frances Densmore made no bones about her theoretical principles either. In discussing the use of microtonal intervals by Native singers and the implication that their use might imply a musical system more complex than that of Europeans, she observes: "To believe this would imply that that they, who are so far behind us in general development, have a musical proficiency far in advance of our own. . . . In these instances it was an evidence of lack of musical development rather than a sign of a high degree of culture . . . the same is true of the rhythmic combinations which characterize the musical performances not only of Indians but of uncultured peoples of distant lands" (1915:187–97).

Until the late 1890s, theories of cultural evolutionary stages went unchallenged as the primary example by which studies of indigenous American cultures were organized, at times in tandem with Clark Wissler's theories of cultural diffusion (chapter 1). It took Franz Boas to break the stranglehold of CES on the American scientific community by proposing alternative concepts that he termed "cultural relativism." For Boas, societies were to be viewed as cultural systems and studied on an individual basis, with careful attention to how lifeways were adapted to unique environments.

Although it took decades for Boas's ideas to filter into the ethnomusicological mainstream, his influence gradually changed how music and culture were thought of in general. George Herzog, a student of Boas who studied language, oral traditions, and music in the Pacific Northwest, in turn taught David McAllester, Alan Merriam, and Bruno Nettl, all of whom did work in the area of Indian music. That trio of prominent scholars were central to moving the discipline of ethnomusicology into the mainstream of the academic world during the 1940s and 1950s, and their work and ideas have influenced generations of scholars who study Indian music. In spite of the virtual disappearance of CES, however, the theory of diffusionism, which dates back to the 1880s, survives almost unchanged and unchallenged. Diffusionism is closely related to the German concept of "culture circles." Instead of a custom or artifact spreading outward from a central point in ever-widening circles, however, diffusionism maintains that cultural knowledge is distributed almost mechanically from one point to another, similar to the way a tree branches.

Since the 1950s, most students of American Indian cultures have regarded learning the classification system known as culture-area theory as the starting point in understanding the vast diversity of Native life-ways. This theory recognizes that environment and geographic proxim-ity determine some general aspects of human material culture and be-havior. As used by Native music specialists, culture areas assist in understanding and categorizing different kinds of songs, vocal styles, mu-sical instruments, and dance types held in common by groups inhabit-ing a particular geographic area. Until the early 1930s, analyses of Indi-an music centered primarily on the repertories of specific tribal groups or regions, such as the Northern Great Plains. It was not until 1936, when Helen H. Roberts published *Musical Areas in Aboriginal North America*, that comparative culture-area theory was applied to the entire North American continent as a broader framework. Roberts identified five large "vocal music areas" (27), although the geographical divisions have since been reconsidered. Culture-area theory is a useful classroom teaching tool, but it, too, has a number of drawbacks that become evi-dent when studying pan-Indian musical genres. Often the Northern and Southern Plains are conflated, with unfortunate results, into a single musical area. Because "all Plains music sounds alike," studies of South-ern Plains musical expression are scarce within the larger body of schol-arship about Native North American music, especially when compared to the amount of work done on Northern Plains people. This does a dis-service to Oklahoma Plains music, which not only has many distinctive repertories but also is the point of origin for much of today's pan-Indian pow-wow music and dance.

I have included this survey of theory and literature stretching back more than a century to make a point: Ethnomusicologists who write about Native North American music must contend with a scholarly tra-dition all their own that contains equal amounts of enviable resources and racialized rationales. And in doing so, they must constantly strain facts from theories and read earlier work with a critical eye.

Few book-length, scholarly studies specifically discuss pan-Indian pow-wows; none focus exclusively on Northern music and dance.[4] Pre-vious writing with some inclusion of musical expression has tended to focus on the Northern Plains and prairie states such as Minnesota. Even less has been written about the Southern style of music, although a num-ber of good ethnographies focusing on Oklahoma Indian cultures in gen-eral do exist.[5] The lack of information on pow-wow music is surprising considering that it is undoubtedly the most widespread contemporary form of Indian musical expression.

Theoretical and Methodological Perspectives

For most ethnomusicologists, including myself, a certain amount of conflict is inherent between theory and method. Expressed at its most basic level, the problem is, Do strongly held theoretical notions alter our methods so we (perhaps unwittingly) custom fit our findings to our theories? At the same time, however, can we legitimately refer to our work in the field as having a method if it lacks a preconceived theoretical perspective? According to Paul Feyerabend (1993), a scholar in the field of the philosophy of science, the answer is clear: There can be no facts without theories. For someone conducting research in the area of Native American music, that stance creates a dilemma. If fact does not exist without theory, how then does one separate the two when considering earlier work?

Considering that almost every paradigm the discipline accepts as "theory" is informed by a Western understanding of how the world works, I picked the lesser of two evils (for me anyway). With deliberately self-limited ideas of what my theoretical model might be, I embarked upon my fieldwork. Boldly risking naiveté, I selected the most emic of methods and for the most part write about music and dance as I have experienced them. Even so, some might object to my use of the term *fieldwork* (or *method* for that matter), because my method went beyond the standard of participant-observer. For ten years, I danced at pow-wows with friends (participation) and watched the dancing when those in my category were not supposed to dance (observation). I also listened to pow-wow music, both live at pow-wows and on my truck's compact disc player when driving cross-country. The closest this comes to a method is the old "bi-musicality" model, except that I do not sit at a Drum and sing—I dance.

That does not mean I lack a theoretical perspective on pow-wow music and dance. Every pow-wow musician and dancer constantly uses theoretical critique when they perform or when they watch and listen to others perform—especially at "contest" pow-wows, where dancers are judged by other dancers (usually competitors in other dance categories) and Drums by other singers. Many standards are universally acknowledged in some way, whereas others are contested, notably when it comes to regalia and dance footwork style. Participants are notorious for being critical of change until after they themselves have adopted it. Other modes of knowledge—such as kinesthetic skill—are conscious but not necessarily verbal. Dancers often explain the character of their footwork through physical demonstration rather than words.

Historical musicologists, recognizing that Beethoven and Brahms did not intentionally connect subdominant to dominant to tonic so theorists could more easily analyze their work a century later, have coined the term *unconscious theory* to describe the internal aesthetic sense that told composers what sounded good and what did not. Pow-wow musicians and dancers are no different. There are internal (and external during compe-tition) sets of standards that define good regalia design, footwork, and musical performance, and they vary regionally to a certain extent. Wheth-er I was dancing, watching other dancers, or listening to the Drums, these unconscious theories constantly informed my pow-wow experience. Therefore, ascertaining what these theories are and clarifying them is one strategy I will pursue throughout this text. How I present much of this information is a step beyond personal interpretation, because, to put it bluntly, in the pow-wow world some things just are the way they are. Many protocols of dress, dance, music, and behavior are explained from within tradition. To try and analyze, for example, why pow-wows grind to a halt when an eagle feather is dropped would border on disrespect to the participants. I can describe what happens and include one or more of the stories told about eagle feathers in my narrative. To go past that point and examine the event through the lens of Western-style theory, howev-er, would strip it of its mystery and power.

Having acknowledged that much of my fieldwork took place while I was dancing and gossiping with friends at pow-wows, I will also admit to often taking notes and talking to other dancers, musicians, commit-tee members, traders, and the audience while attending but not dancing at various events. Coordinating pow-wow attendance with grant-fund-ing, my work was structured in a way that allowed me to conduct a multi-site ethnography. I surveyed numerous traditional and competition pow-wows from the Michigan-Wisconsin region and the Northern Great Plains, contrasting music, dancer interaction, overall set-up of dance are-nas, and insider-outsider perceptions at specific events. Over the four summers from 1996 to 1999 I conducted fieldwork at eight pow-wows in Michigan and South Dakota and interviewed two extended families, one an Ojibwe-Ottawa family from Michigan and the other an Oglala Lakota family from the Pine Ridge Reservation. During that time I made very few field recordings of music. Out of consideration for musicians, I either purchased recordings directly from them (my first choice), from pow-wow traders (my second choice), or from a dealer who had a good reputation in Indian Country, such as Drumbeat Indian Arts. Everyone who worked with me, from the youngsters who helped lug gear to the long-time friends I interviewed, was paid an honorarium from one of my grants. Most of these people did not expect or demand payment but were given such as a gesture of respect for the value of their knowledge.

The people who participated as consultants in this project are all friends of at least ten years, and our relationship is a reverse of the usual academic-informant paradigm. Social hierarchies in place during ethnomusicological research often result in inequalities between academics and consultants. In this case, however, everyone with whom I worked is above me on the pow-wow social scale. They are all far better dancers and singers than I and have national reputations; I am a small-time, small pow-wow dancer. Unlike some scholars who conduct research in a foreign country and then return to their native land to publish and teach, I continue to participate—sometimes sporadically—in pow-wows, feeling lucky if I make the finals in a group of only four or five other contestants.

Writing and Reader Response

Even after seven years of dancing, it was not until the early stages of writing the manuscript for this book that I began to think about the roots of pow-wow–specific (as opposed to generic, pan-Indian) "culture." What makes pow-wows distinctive enough from each other that a Dance in one region can be radically unlike another only five hundred miles away, even when the structures of dances, songs, and order of events are practically identical? These questions framed my inquiry, and I concentrated on a specific style of pow-wow—Northern—and two primary regions, the Great Plains and the Great Lakes, in an effort to create a cohesive, comparative structure. Then, after moving from Wisconsin to California in 1995, I realized that in order to discuss Northern-style music, the Southern musical tradition would need presentation as well. Perhaps my most difficult consideration concerned who a typical reader might be. That single question more than any other would shape my narrative.

Writing for two sets of readers—academic and Native—requires fluency and respect for multiple musical languages and the ability to navigate a political minefield. Ownership of non-material culture is critical to North American Indians, who perceive the gradual erosion of cultural knowledge as the latest in a series of threats to their survival as distinct people. Control of the discourse about culture is seen as one way to assert cultural sovereignty, and publications on Indian subjects are increasingly subject to critique in such Native American and Canadian publications as *Aboriginal Voices*, *News from Indian Country*, and *Indian Country Today*. Even more troubling from a scholar's perspective is the trend toward political fragmentation and infighting within tribal groups (or even families) over control of musical knowledge and the right to present it publicly. For example, in 1996 members of a southern California reservation's Cultural Conservation Committee visited the music library at the University of California, Los Angeles, demanding repatriation of materials found in a 1955 music education master's thesis. Committee members claimed that the thesis contained restricted knowledge that should not be available to the public. Upon further investigation, I discovered that the committee was made up of tribal members belonging to a specific political faction whose method of gaining power was to "corner the market" on cultural—specifically, musical—knowledge and that the "public" was, in fact, another faction within the tribe.

In the past, most writing on indigenous American music has been aimed at a non-Indian audience, but that is changing. *Songs and Dances of the Lakota* (1976) by Ben Black Bear and R. D. Thiesz, intended primarily for adult Indian (in this case, Lakota) readers, uses nontechnical language and diagrams to describe musical form and history. The songtexts themselves are presented in bilingual format, and Lakota song histories and texts are paired, page by page, with their English translations. Judith Vander's *Songprints: The Musical Experience of Five Shoshone Women* (1988) represents another shift from the Western theoretical-analytical approach. Much of its text is dialogic, which allows readers to "hear" Native voices directly and unfiltered by layers of interpretation. Vander clearly separates her commentaries from those of her consultants, and Western-style history and analysis is defined by blocks of type. In *The Power of Kiowa Song: A Collaborative Ethnography* (1998), Luke Lassiter takes yet another approach and writes himself directly into the narrative. Before the book's publication, Kiowa collaborators approved large sections of the text. The drawback to this style of personal narrative, similar to those described by Mary Louise Pratt (1986) is that it can too often be perceived as self-indulgent. It also takes control of the final manuscript—something I am unwilling to relinquish—from the author.

Two models, one from anthropology and the other from ethnomusicology, caught my interest as I moved forward with actually writing about my experiences and putting my field notes into a semblance of a rough draft. The first, as described by Pratt (1986:193), suggests forming ethnographic pairs that consist of formal ethnographies and personal narratives. James Clifford (1988:50) posits an even more radical model:

> One increasingly common way to manifest the collaborative production of ethnographic knowledge is to quote regularly and at length from informants. . . . But such a tactic only begins to break up monophonic au-

thority. Quotations are always staged by the quoter and tend to serve merely as examples or confirming testimonies. Looking beyond quotation, one might imagine a more radical polyphony that would "do the natives and the ethnographer in different voices"; but this would only displace ethnographic authority, still confirming the final virtuoso orchestration by a single author of all the discourses in his or her text.

In contrast, Michael Bakan, an ethnomusicologist, has suggested an "alternative ethnomusicology in which [a] culture's authority over music is decentered in ways that allow for the subject positions of all experiencers and potential experiencers of any music to be treated as ethnomusicologically relevant" (1999:13). Bakan is a Western-trained musician, and his approach holds great appeal for me because it implies that my transcriptions and analytical diagrams are but one way of many to experience pow-wows and no less valid than the experiences of pow-wow singers themselves. Reversing this scenario, in 1989 I invited some Cherokee and Pawnee friends to a Denver concert of Beethoven's Ninth Symphony, in which I was playing the timpani. It was the first time that any of them had attended a formal concert of Western art music, and from everything they said afterward they found it a thoroughly enjoyable affair. As Beethoven novices, was their experience of the performance any less valid than mine? I think not. Mine was probably more intensely moment by moment than theirs, because I was counting measures and playing while they had the luxury of relaxation (and the ability to hear the strings over the brass). Yet neither encounter with the music had more validity than the other.

Following Clifford and Pratt, I have framed this text as an "ethnographic pair." My formal narrative and analysis will be in the first four chapters and those of my consultants, in a dialogic mode, in the final two. My hope is that by dovetailing dialogic methodologies with those of Western theoretical discourse (rather than dispersing them throughout the text) I can foreground consultants' voices in a way that makes them equal to mine. In the more formally analytical chapters, I will use Western methods of analysis but also include indigenous musical concepts and structures. Indian musicians do not talk about song-making in a densely analytical way, but then again neither do most musicians outside the academy. What Indian musicians do talk about is process, which involves personal (sometimes tribal) history, tradition, song function, and the immediacy of performance. With that in mind, I have worked toward a bi-analytical style in the formal text, incorporating and privileging Native musical thought and including narratives from pow-wow singers and dancers in tandem with scholarly literature.

Recognizing the emic-etic knowledge binary, a bi-analytical approach presents the understandings and interpretations of both realms as equally valid. During interviews with singers and dancers, for example, I often use a dual Western and Native musical vocabulary in the course of my questioning. "What is the tempo or speed of your songs?" and "Do you compose/write/make songs?" allows musicians to choose among a variety of terms rather than having a vocabulary imposed upon them. Consultants interpret and clarify comments as we converse, knowingly speaking directly to a reading public, and receive transcribed copies of interviews with the right to remove or edit as they see fit. Interviews are in the form of a conversation. By placing myself within the narrative rather than above I am able to avoid the inference that I possess more knowledge about pow-wow song creation than those who actually make songs.

As Clifford suggested, these sessions are presented in chapters 6 and 7 and with minimal interpretation on my part. Every person who speaks through these interviews has far more expertise in his or her area of music and dance than I do. Stories told by the two families have a life and intensity all their own and should be heard as they tell them. For me to cut, paste, edit, and interpret assumes that Indians are incapable of understanding the realities of communicating to a larger audience.

A bi-analytical methodology also allows me to assign specific information and opinions to specific individuals. By working with these consultants, I am designating them as culture-bearers; they, too, should accept responsibility within the larger Indian community for what they have said. By the same token, I have left my sections of the dialog relatively intact, retaining the idiom I use in everyday conversations outside the academy. This was a conscious decision on my part, stemming from a desire to present not only my fieldwork experience but also myself.

The larger topic of pow-wows is divided into five subfields throughout the narrative, broadly categorized as:

1. Western historical/literary review: Brief surveys of ethnographic research and anthropological theory as relating to American Indians.
2. Native oral histories: Excerpts from historical narratives, as recorded by ethnologists, and contemporary Indian oral histories.
3. Western terminology, transcriptions, and analyses: Pow-wow music as seen through the lens of Western-style analysis and notation.
4. Native terminology and analyses: Pow-wow music and dance discussed using the medium of contemporary pan-Indian discourse.
5. Native history and compositional process: Unedited, loosely structured interviews with pow-wow dancers and musicians.

The text that follows includes anthropological and Western histori-cal documentation, bits of oral tradition, transcriptions using both aca-demic and Indian terminology and analysis, narratives from Indian sing-ers, and my interpretations in an attempt to present this music honestly and from multiple perspectives, giving justice to each. In no sense do I expect to "teach" Indian pow-wow participants much of anything, nor is that my primary goal. For the most part, pow-wow singers and danc-ers know perfectly well how their music and dance works and what it means, and they do not need me to tell them about it. Rather, my aim is to document pow-wow life at a particular time and place for the Native community so future generations have better understanding of what Dances were like at turn of the twentieth century, an issue Shannon Martin addresses at the end of chapter 6. If the first few chapters provide pow-wow committees with decent historical information to "borrow" for their programs, so much the better.

My hope is that this text will offer non-Indian readers an entry point into a richly textured realm of music and dance. Pow-wow announcers are usually very much in tune with the nuances of explaining dance style and history to audiences unfamiliar with both. When it comes to music, however, the system often breaks down. Non-Indians may appreciate pow-wow music for its aural qualities alone, but to best understand it they need to comprehend its structure and how closely dance and song fit together. In the late 1980s, for example, a friend—a renowned orchestral musician—told me how he and his wife enjoyed going to pow-wows, but he could not make heads or tails of the music. His wife confided that he would stand next to the Drums as they performed, listen intently, and come back shak-ing his head. Although I drew out a basic, Western-style diagram for him, I suspect the music's structure did not sink in until he sat in the front row at a pow-wow music and dance workshop I taught at the American Mu-sicological Society meeting in 1997. That audience—musically knowl-edgeable non-Indians who enjoy pow-wows—is one I feel a special respon-sibility to serve. Although the vocabulary used in the analysis that follows may be meaningless to Indian readers from a performance perspective, my employment of Western terminology to clarify musical structures fits well into the tradition of "sharing the culture." One aspect of pow-wows, af-ter all, involves reaching out to all those in attendance.

By introducing all relevant sources relating to music history, analy-sis, composition/making, and performance, I intend to mediate the dis-tance between Western scholarship and Native understanding. Although an academic, I am also a pow-wow dancer of Oklahoma Choctaw (paternal) and, to a lesser degree, Grand River Mohawk (maternal) ancestry. Pow-wows are not an integral part of Choctaw culture the way they are to the Southern Plains people. Although some Choctaws do dance, I did not go to pow-wows regularly until I was in my twenties. When I was a young teenager, however, I did attend two with my grandfather—one at the Sherman Indian School in Riverside, California, and another in Bishop, California. At Bishop, Grandpa bought me a fancy pair of moccasins, reminding me to "never forget my Indian blood." For me, pow-wows always recall that moment.

The bulk of my formal musical training has been as an orchestral percussionist, with some lessons on violin, piano, and organ thrown in. Another part of my childhood musical life did, I think, make moving into the pow-wow circle much easier for me than it has been for many others. My childhood was filled with music because my mother loved to sing. My sister and I learned thirty to forty American folksongs by ear when we were children. As an adult, I learned to hear pow-wow songs the same way, by listening and humming along and later singing along to tapes I bought from traders. Learning the music by reading it was never an option, so I was lucky that I had a good ear and could pick up melodies and internalize entire songs. And just as I never thought analytically about the songs of my childhood, I never moved pow-wow songs through the systematic realm of my musical perception. As a result, now I find myself hearing music in an Indian way (round, honor beat, word song) when dancing and in a Western way (strophe, accent, vocable) while transcribing and writing. In a very real sense, my musical experience as a dancer and academic mirrors the indigenous concept of complementarity or "twinness" as described by Beverly Diamond, Sam Cronk, and Franziska von Rosen (1994:17–42). By presenting in this text Indian and Western musical conceptualizations as dualities rather than as oppositional stances, my intention is that a meeting place between the two can be created, something a Navajo friend who is also an academic calls the "middle way."

I would remind readers, especially those familiar with pow-wow traditions, that it is not possible to tell everyone's story. Illustrating the pitfalls of single-perspective presentation of Indian cultural knowledge is an anecdote in which names have not been changed because we all know who we are. In the summer of 1987, I got a call from my friend Norma asking me to come and help out in making fry-bread for a big feed up at the Native American Rights Fund (NARF) offices that evening. When I got over to Thunderbird Apartments, Norma—who is Lakota—and another friend, Roberta—who is Navajo—were busily making fry-bread in two different apartments. The doors of both units were wide open, and thick, black smoke was billowing out into the parking lot. Norma and Roberta had been arguing about which kind of fry-bread was better, Lakota-style or Navajo-style, and decided that I would be the judge after the cooking was through. While I was helping Norma with fry-bread cooking by turning over bread and stacking it in a cooler, she spent time explaining to me all the wonders of Lakota fry-bread—its versatility and how it could easily be reheated in a microwave after sitting around for awhile, and then it would taste almost as good as new. Navajo fry-bread, she said, "tastes like crackers after maybe fifteen minutes." After carefully rehearsing me for the moment of tasting truth, Norma and I went out into the parking lot with coolers full of fry-bread. Then Norma and Roberta each handed me a small piece of their bread. But before I could say "Lakota bread is better," Roberta put her hands around my throat and started to squeeze while lifting at the same time—just like Darth Vader. "Just say, Navajo fry-bread is better," she said. And I did.

Just as with fry bread taste concepts, conflicting narratives about pow-wow origins and practices abound, at times forcing me to choose which version I present. This does periodically result in a single perspective—mine—being presented as a kind of "truth." Just as pow-wow traditions come from many Nations, there are also many truths, and I make no claims to being the ultimate authority on pow-wows. This book is a beginning not an end, and I hope it is only the first of many texts celebrating the vibrancy, continuity, and evolution of North America's oldest music and dance tradition.

2 People and Histories

As I began researching the origins of pow-wows, conflicts among the pow-wow origin narratives of different tribal communities became increasingly evident and problematic. Although clearly there is no single birthplace of the pow-wow, scores of tribes claim to have held the "first."[1] Rather than become entangled in this debate, I intend to present the various strands of music and dance culture that have joined together to create the contemporary pow-wow, including warrior society dances, reservation-era intertribal dances, Wild West shows and other exhibitions, and postwar homecoming celebrations. Even today, pow-wows come in a myriad of forms, including contest and traditional dance-only events; "homecomings," which are veteran-centered and often include parades; "fairs," where the pow-wow is only part of a program that includes a carnival and a rodeo; and "picnics," an Oklahoma term for a smaller, more region-specific Dance.

Because pow-wow origins are a contested topic in Indian circles, presenting every Northern tribe's pow-wow history is well beyond the scope of this study. Instead, I will cover a limited series of significant historical issues, beginning with a broad survey and critique of the literature about the Omaha/Grass Dance styles (generally considered to be the precursor to most men's pow-wow dances) and finishing with a brief case study of a single event. Between these two points, my focus will be on circumstances that shaped contemporary forms of intertribalism and the Lakota and Anishnaabeg people whose pow-wow traditions are central to this narrative.

History, Research, and Oral Traditions

The first comprehensive Western discussion of the spread across the Great Plains of the ancestral forms of modern pow-wow music and dance—then known as the Grass (or Omaha/O'ho-ma) Dance "complex"—was Clark Wissler's "General Discussion of Shamanistic and Dancing Societies" (1916). Wissler traces the spread of the dance complex through the diffusion of its regalia, selected ceremonial objects, and specific ritual actions, and although he makes no mention of music, his work is still the gold standard of reference for those who write about pow-wow music and its origins. Among those who have cited Wissler are Hatton (1986:199–200), Vander (1988:43–46), and Vennum (1984:54–55).

One of my greatest concerns over a decade of researching the influence of Wissler's work has been how his written materials have steadily infiltrated and pushed aside Native oral traditions about dance origins, primarily through the printed programs of pow-wows. Wissler's account, organized using the mechanical, nineteenth-century theory of diffusionism, has been steadily quoted and retold in scholarly texts. Far too often, reports from written sources are repeated enough times that they eventually fold into existing oral traditions. Wissler's study has done just that and has collapsed the Grass/Omaha Dance of 1900 into the Grass Dance of 2000. Much of this confusion is due to a misunderstanding and conflation of terminology and the fact that there are two Grass Dances, one a Northern Plains style of men's pow-wow dancing and the other an ancestral version of what is known as the Men's Northern Traditional Dance.

Grass dancing, as seen at today's pow-wows, is a young man's dance, athletic, strenuous, and with a unique style of footwork found in no other form of Native dancing. The dancer moves in a controlled, falling motion, shoulders swaying as his feet "flatten the grass." William Powers, an anthropologist and specialist in Lakota linguistics, relates one version of how the dance came by its name: "Basically, the Grass Dance is the same as the Omaha Dance of the Sioux . . . the war dance of the plains. The name 'Grass Dance' comes from the custom of some tribes wearing braided grass in their belts to symbolize the scalps of their enemies. Among the Sioux, the older form of dance was called *peji ipiyaka ogna wacipi* (they dance with the grass in their belts). The Sioux of North Dakota nowadays call the dance simply *Peji Waci* or Grass Dance" (1963:1). Severt Young Bear tells a similar tale, however, he differentiates between Grass and Omaha dancing: "They [Grass dancers] have their own set of songs and their dancers do a lot of fancy footwork. They dance backwards, cross their legs, and go in circles. By comparison, the Omaha and tokala [Kit Fox Warrior Society] dancers were straight dancers" (Young Bear and Theisz 1994:56). In 1989 Norma Rendon (Oglala Lakota) provided an account that differs from Powers's: "Grass Dance originated a ways back. The Lakota, a long time ago they had these men, and they would wear a row of grass around their head, around their arms, around their ankles and right under their knees. . . . As they [the dancers after returning from a successful raid or war party] went into the dance arena before the People, they would stomp down the grass with their feet."

Rendon's version explains the distinctive footwork of contemporary Grass dancers, so unlike that of the traditional Omaha or warrior society dancer. More significant in scholarly circles, however, is Powers's statement that Grass and Omaha dancing are the same thing with different names.[2] If so, Wissler's hypothesis of the diffused Great Plains Grass Dance complex extends to the present and aligns with the contemporary reading that old-style Grass/Omaha dancing was the basis of all modern men's pow-wow dancing and regalia. But what then of Rendon's account, based upon a Lakota oral tradition? Is it conceivable that the ancestral forms of Grass and Omaha Dances were distinct and had a single, overlapping musical style, generically referred to "Omaha" or War Dance songs? Indian terminology can sometimes be deceptive to outsiders, with a single word having multiple and hidden meanings.

Wissler maintains that the earliest form of Grass dancing came from the Pawnee around 1820, who called the dance Iruska (the fire is in me) (Murie 1914:608).[3] The Iruska Dance—generically known as a "Hot Dance"—had as its focal point the act of drawing meat chunks from a boiling kettle. During the 1830s, the Pawnee gave (or sold) the Iruska to the Omaha/Ponca Nation, which referred to their version of the dance/ritual as the Heluska (Man Dance). In the early 1840s, the Omaha sold the right to perform the dance and its songs to the Yanktonai Dakota, who soon after gave performance rights to the Teton Lakota. Both nations called the ceremony "Omaha Dance" in honor of the people from whom they had bought it. From the Lakota, Omaha dancing "diffused" over the Northern Plains, where most tribes that performed it began to call it the Grass Dance.

The Pawnee Iruska is, as are most Plains male dances, associated with a warrior society. According to Pawnee oral tradition, the dance was received through a vision by a man named Crow-Feather. While Crow-Feather was in a trancelike state, the spirits gifted him with a porcupine and deer-hair roach and a crow bustle or "belt." A roach is a crest of stiff porcupine guard hairs with a deer-hair center that male dancers wear on their heads; a bustle is the spray of feathers worn on their backs. Crow belts, a specific type of bustle made from the carcass of a crow, wings spread, are the precursors of the more formalized eagle-feather bustles used today.

In addition to the regalia items, Crow-Feather received special medicines (spiritual powers) enabling him to pull chunks of meat from a boiling kettle without burning himself, a gesture that imitates the act of hunters pulling steaming entrails from the stomachs of newly killed game. An important part of any vision is its uniqueness, and we should assume that the Pawnee had never used the roach and crow belt—at least not in this combination or specific style—that came to them for the first time through Crow-Feather's vision. In addition to goods and medicines, the spirits also granted Crow-Feather forty songs to sing during the Iruska ceremony, and he was to be accompanied by four men playing water drums. Because the Pawnee, a Southern tribe of Caddoan cultural origins, moved to the area of modern-day Nebraska after 1750, it is entirely possible that they were unfamiliar with regalia items more common to the Northern Plains and to prairie people.

When the Pawnee gave the right to form this warrior society to the Omaha/Ponca Nation (at that time a single tribe that also claimed to have originated the society), the four water drums were replaced by a single large drum, commonly referred to as the "big drum." Ornamental whips, and in some cases one or two U.S. Army swords, were added to the ceremonial regalia. Based on a study of the spread of these items, the roach, and the crow belt, Wissler concluded that he was tracing the diffusion of the Omaha/Grass Dance as a song/dance ritual entity. He makes no mention, however, of what the dance looked like in terms of footwork, how its accompanying songs sounded, or the specific purposes behind many of the ceremony's ritual actions.

It is difficult to trace the dispersion of a warrior society around the Great Plains through a study of the spread of regalia and a few linguistic similarities. One problem shows up in the narrative of an unknown Lakota man recorded by Thomas Tyon (also Lakota) around 1900. According to Tyon's informant, there were a number of warrior societies in each Indian nation, and all had similar regalia (Walker 1980:265). In addition, Wissler failed to differentiate among regalia indigenous to each tribe and articles introduced from the outside, such as swords, iron cooking kettles, and perhaps even the big drum he claims to be the Omaha's major contribution to the society. These external objects were all cultural leveling devices. To numerous outsiders many dances appear identical, especially when observers are distracted by the more colorful aspects of a ceremony. Combined with the basic similarities of Plains Indian regalia, external elements masked salient differences among warrior societies.

Such confusion fostered the illusion of the Heluska/Omaha/Grass Dance Society as the single major pan-tribal Plains warrior society after 1880, although many other societies had similar regalia. Adding to the confusion was the proclivity of Victorian-era white Americans to assume that a surface sameness in dance style and regalia was a marker for similarities in ritual action and social function. Comments by Helen Marie Bennett, the superintendent of schools in Deadwood, South Dakota, are representative of that mindset.[4] "The Omaha," she noted, "is the only dance now practiced among the Sioux" (1902:346). Bennett made these remarks at about the same time as Tyon's informant was describing numerous warrior societies.

Two major items of Heluska regalia, the crow belt and the roach, were commonly found on the Northern Plains well before the advent of the Omaha Dance. A number of paintings by George Catlin show that the Lakota used crow belts in the Beggars Dance of 1832, almost thirty years before they purchased rights to the Omaha Dance, its regalia, and its songs (McCracken 1959:45). In addition, museum specimens of roaches (although of the round style) from the Great Lakes area date from 1800 (Phillips 1987:62). Because the roach was also part of the regalia of the Kit Fox Society, it was undoubtedly part of Lakota warriors' regalia before the coming of the Omaha Dance (Walker 1980:following 226). The war insignia of the Kit Fox Society bears a striking resemblance to that worn in an early photograph of another man who is labeled as an Omaha dancer (Walker 1980:following 194).

Other than dance regalia, Wissler's major evidence of the Omaha society's diffusion is constructed from an analysis of Native language terms, specifically those used to describe the ritual actions in the part of the ceremony that culminates with snatching pieces of meat from a kettle of boiling water. These actions are a central part of the Pawnee Iruska, Omaha Hethushka [sic], and Lakota Heyoka (Heyo'ka) ceremonies. Wissler (1916:861, 859) glosses the three ceremony names (Iruska, Hethushka, and Heyoka) as having identical origins and meanings (finding them to have derived from the Pawnee Hot Dance custom of taking boiling meat from a kettle), but only after first crediting the origination of the same ritual action to the Dakota. Following that logic, Wissler suggests that the Dakota, Nakota, and Lakota had this portion of the ceremony first, and it spread from those nations to the Pawnee after the Siouian tribes adopted Pawnee terminology. Because that chain of events was played out over thousands of square miles and among hostile tribal entities, the hypothesis does not hold up well under scrutiny.

Although the Pawnee Iruska ceremony did involve snatching chunks of meat from a kettle of boiling water, other tribes performed exactly the same act as part of one or more of their ceremonies—and for entirely different purposes. The practice is not confined to the Plains; northeastern Iroquois perform the same gesture as part of a curing "doing." Pulling boiling hot meat from a kettle, a ritual common to all Hot Dance ceremonies, might to an outsider imply diffusion from a single originating event. Although physically it is the same act, it has different contextual meaning within warrior society ceremonials than it does in dream society rituals and teachings. Moreover, any Plains Indian of the nineteenth century would have been well aware of each warrior society's distinct nature and tribal purpose and of the differences between a warrior society and a dream society such as the Lakota Heyoka.

In Lakota culture, the Heyo'ka is a dream society, something very different in nature from the Pawnee Iruska or Omaha Hethushka (both warrior societies). Membership in a warrior society is generally based upon a demonstration of valor in battle. For the most part, although not exclusively, warriors in nineteenth-century Plains culture were male. Therefore, with the exception of women who performed specific ceremonial duties, membership in warrior societies was made up of men, although in modern Plains culture female veterans are more common and more likely to be included. Conversely, the Heyo'ka dream society was more loosely organized and open to all who dreamed of Thunderbeings, regardless of gender (although women were rare). The element of pulling hot meat from a kettle had different meaning in this ceremonial context. Rather than proving stoic endurance, as Wissler contends, it was a display of the contrary nature of a Heyo'ka dreamer, who would loudly proclaim that the meat was extremely cold after pulling it from the boiling water. The word *heyoka* means "contrary," and the society has little connection to bravery in battle. Rather, the Lakota Heyo'ka, though personal humiliation and invocation of metaphorical tribal knowledge, teaches people to recognize and acknowledge their connections with the natural world.

Wissler footnotes (but otherwise ignores) versions of the Grass Dance origin story different from his. As Stephen Riggs, a missionary and Dakota-English dictionary author, describes the Dakota Grass Dance, "It is said to have derived its name from the custom, in ancient times, of dancing naked or with only a wisp of grass around the loins. It is a night dance and regarded as extremely licentious" (1894:227). In a study conducted three years after Wissler's, ethnologist Frances Densmore took down clues to the possible beginnings of what is now the contemporary (pow-wow–style) Grass Dance among the Lakota. Influenced by Wissler, however, she failed fully to grasp what she saw. Referring to a photograph labeled "Omaha Dancers," Densmore states (1918:470), "Mr. Higheagle said that two kinds of grass dance are now danced on the Standing Rock Reservation—the old men's grass dance and the young men's. The former is shown . . . [in] a photograph taken several years ago on the reservation and identified by Mr. Higheagle. The view undoubtedly presents some of the old features of the dance which have been changed by the present generation."

Wissler also concluded that the Omaha society was reserved for mature, experienced warriors (1916:866). Yet contemporary Grass dancing is a strenuous dance performed by younger men. Perhaps the same custom existed in the 1800s, but there were two entirely separate dances—one purchased from the Omaha and the other an indigenous Lakota form—rather than only one dance changed by young men, as Densmore claims.

In Densmore's photograph of the Omaha Dance, a group of men dance with stiff, upright upper body postures and wear feather bustles not bunches or braids of grass. Their regalia and bearing are much closer to the modern Traditional dancer than the Grass dancer (for an image of a dancer from this period, see photograph 1). Contemporary Grass dancers wear no bustle and instead sew yarn or chainette fringe on their regalia to represent grass. In a photograph labeled "Omaha Dance," taken on the Pine Ridge Reservation in 1891 (more than a decade before the one Densmore describes), some dancers wear bunches—not braids—of grass tied around their waists, which conforms to Rendon's description (Walker 1980:following page 194). Perhaps even then there were two different dances with two fashions of regalia, and there was a single name for both. Those unfamiliar with the distinctions may have been confused by the similar terminology and conflated the two.

Typical contemporary Northern Traditional dance regalia includes a roach topped (ideally) with two eagle feathers, a bone-pipe breastplate, an eagle feather bustle, and a feather fan (made from bird-of-prey feathers) held in the left hand. All of these items were elements of the old Omaha dancer's regalia, but all were also used by most warrior societies. In contrast, the regalia of contemporary pow-wow Grass dancers is trimmed with yarn, which symbolizes grass. They also wear a roach topped with eagle feathers or fluffs (said to represent clouds) but not a breastplate or bustle of any kind. The regalia for a third, and related, variety of men's dancing, Oklahoma-style Southern Straight, also lacks a bustle but includes feather fan and often a roach.

In describing the music of the contemporary Lakota Grass Dance, Powers states that these songs are differentiated from traditional Lakota dance songs by a lack of what he terms a "Sioux yelp" (in Lakota, the *a'kisa*). He also finds that distinction is the key to proving that Grass Dance songs came from outside the Lakota repertoire, probably from the Omaha (Powers 1963:1).[5] He ignores, however, the difference between simple vocal embellishment style and the larger, more formal elements of modern pow-wow songs. "Sioux yelp" or not, all the songs have been made using an identical form.

Even if Powers is correct about the "yelp" aspect of Grass Dance songs and about the traditional singing style for Grass Dance songs coming to the Lakota from the Omaha, it does not automatically follow that the dance itself did. Because form and beat pattern are identical in Grass Dance and Omaha Dance songs, it is just as reasonable to conclude that "Omaha Dance" refers to song form, meter, and accent patterns and "Grass Dance" to Lakota-specific footwork and regalia style. A thorough reading of the literature suggests that the principle sources of confusion regarding Grass and Omaha dancing come from innumerable non-Indian observers who have identified all Lakota dances as Omaha dances rather than all Lakota dance songs as Omaha-form songs. It is also possible that least some Indians grew tired of explaining their dances to outside spectators and called all the dances "Grass" or "Omaha."

The nineteenth-century Omaha Dance as a footwork and regalia style has been absorbed (in the North) into the modern category of the men's Northern Traditional Dance (which includes parts of many old warrior society dances). It does not resemble either contemporary Grass dancing or the historic version of the Lakota "young man's" Grass Dance. Side-by-side comparisons of period photographs reveal that the two dances do not look the same and were not performed historically by the same age groups—although they might have employed songs that had similar formal structures. The Grass Dance of Wissler's treatise is not the Grass Dance of the contemporary pow-wow but rather the ancestral form of what are now called the Northern Traditional styles. That does not mean, however, that the old Omaha version of the Grass/Omaha Dance that Wissler documented has completely vanished from the pow-wow circuit. The Crow Indians of Montana have preserved the old Omaha style in its early-twentieth-century form, calling their version the "Crow" Traditional. These men dance with the same regalia as they did in the 1900s—crow (or mess) bustles, bare legs strung with leg bells, and flattened roaches—just as worn by Northern Plains Omaha/Grass Dancers in photographs from the turn of the century.

Unfortunately, with the wealth of information available from earlier research, anthropologists and ethnomusicologists tend to put aside orally transmitted narratives such as Rendon's in favor of written ethnographic accounts, most (but not all) by cultural outsiders. A typical example of how Wissler's authority plays out in contemporary scholarship comes from Thomas Vennum:

> As the Hethushka model was adapted by other tribes, they called it either the Omaha Dance or Grass Dance. The latter designation was most certainly derived from part of the regalia worn by the Hethushka dancers: a long bunch of grass tied to the back of their belts to symbolize scalps taken in battle. But although the name Grass dance was used, the original significance of the bunch of grass was soon forgotten by the new adherents; or inferred the name's derivation from some local practice of longstanding. Such an explanation was given by the Hidatsa man Edward Goodbird [born ca. 1868] for the origin of the term among his people. (1982:53–54)

Goodbird's story involving warriors carrying and using dry grass to start fires in damp weather may indeed reveal the origins of the Grass Dance in Hidatsa culture. In this case, Vennum, otherwise known for meticulous fieldwork and research, unquestioningly assumes Wissler's accuracy and places it ahead of Goodbird's. Putting aside all of the contradictions in Wissler's writings, the final, and most problematic, facet of his research was its method. Raymond DeMallie, in his introduction to a compilation of James Walker's research notes for Wissler (Walker 1980), reveals that Wissler did little of his own fieldwork, preferring to hire others for the task. In fact, he never saw many of the tribes he wrote about, much less experienced their music and dance.

Pow-wows, Medicine Shows, and the "Wild West"

The term *pow-wow* is probably from the Algonquian language family of the northeastern United States and Canada and derived from the Narragansett words *pau wau*, which gloss as "he/she dreams." Among the first Indian people German immigrants encountered as they began to arrive in the Colonies during the mid-seventeenth century were the various Algonquian-speaking tribes of New England. Folk-healers from European societies gravitated toward Indian healing practices. They appropriated the term *pau wau*, used by Indians to describe specific ritual actions that took place during curing ceremonies, and adopted it to describe the settlers' general use of herbal remedies. Since that time, practitioners of Anglo-American and Pennsylvania German folk medicine (known as "pow-wow doctors") employed the word *pow-wowing* to denote "charms, incantation, magic and laying on of hands for avoiding or curing disease or injury" (Vogel 1970:126). The practitioners were heavily influenced by the customs of Indian traditional healers. Traveling from place to place, they styled themselves as "Indian healers" and sold bottled cure-alls that contained large amounts of alcohol and/or opium. According to Virgil Vogel, in the two decades following the Civil War:

> The most dramatic promotional stunt in the vending of alleged Indian remedies was the medicine show, which once ranked with the circus and chautaqua as a seasonal relief to the monotony of small-town existence. From the post Civil War era until the beginning of World War I, these spectacles toured the country with bands of "real live Indians," pitching their tents in some mud flat and advertising their presence with a noisy and colorful parade down Main Street. Audiences were treated to an exhibition of "war dances" and other nights of the "wild west." (1970:141)

Although non-Indian spectators had been entertained by Indian dances before this time, the use of dancing in tandem with pow-wow doctors resulted in the term *pow-wow* being associated with the concept of "Indians dancing." By the 1880s, Indians themselves (minus the Anglo pow-wow doctors) were putting together intertribal "Indian Medicine shows" and traveling from town to town in the Midwest.

During the heyday of pow-wow doctors and traveling medicine shows, Plains Indians were fighting to save their lands and way of life from destruction. One by one, the tribes of the Great Plains and Southwest were subjugated, cajoled into signing treaties, and forced onto reservations so their lands could be confiscated and opened for non-Indian settlement. In order to "break-up the tribal mass" (and seize more land in the process), the stated policy of the American government became that of forced assimilation though destruction of culture, both material and spiritual. First, religious ceremonies were forbidden. Then, in 1902, the commissioner of Indian affairs issued the first of many edicts forbidding dancing. By the 1920s, dancing on reservations was being severely repressed by Charles H. Burke, the commissioner of Indian affairs during the Coolidge administration (1923–29). As Lawrence Kelly observes, "Like most of his contemporaries, Burke regarded Indian religion as superstitious and backward. While the Indian service could not impose Christianity upon the Indians, Burke believed it should do everything within its power to assist the religious volunteers who worked among the Indians" (1983:259).

The most notorious (in Native circles) of Burke's edicts was Circular 1665, *Indian Dancing* (1921):

> On a number of reservations, however, the native dance still has enough evil tendencies to furnish a retarding influence and at times a trouble-

some situation which calls for careful consideration and right-minded efforts. It is not the policy of the Indian office to denounce all forms of dancing. . . . The dance *per se* is not condemned. . . . The dance, however, under most primitive and pagan conditions, is apt to be harmful, and when found so among the Indians we should control it by educational measures as far as possible, but if necessary, by punitive measures when its degrading tendencies persist. The sun-dance and all other similar dances and so-called religious ceremonies are considered "Indian Offences" under existing regulations, and corrective penalties are provided.

As a follow-up, in 1923 Burke instructed superintendents to limit the duration of Indian dances and put a halt to certain "degrading ceremonials." Indians had little recourse. They were not granted citizenship until 1924 and possessed limited legal rights as wards of the government. Thus dancing either went underground, away from the supervision of Indian agents and missionaries, or was practiced only in such legal forms as entertainment for non-Indians at Wild West and medicine shows or at exhibition dances.

The success of the American government in forcing dancing underground depended largely on how much control the Bureau of Indian Affairs could exert over a specific tribe. Some groups, such as those of the Cherokee, Creek, and Seminole of Oklahoma, were allowed to continue traditional dancing with little interference. Others, such as the Lakota of South Dakota, were more tightly controlled and needed passes from the Indian agent to leave their reservation for travel, a policy that continued into the 1950s (Densmore 1918:4; Rendon interview, Aug. 15, 1989). Because of these policies, Wild West shows and county fair circuits were among the few legal venues where the Lakota and many other Plains people, now poverty-stricken, could dance and earn income.

During the 1890s, both Buffalo Bill's Wild West and Pawnee Bill's show toured the United States and Europe, giving people a close look at the Indians of the now-tamed western frontier. White audiences developed intense curiosity about Indian cultures and flocked to see these colorful theatricals before the "vanishing" Americans vanished permanently. Their fascination with Indians led to the 1898 Omaha exhibition, which "became the precedent for Indian exhibitions sanctioned and paid for by the United States Government" (Young 1981:187).

Through the medium of Wild West shows, some Indian traditions, if presented as entertainment for non-Indians, gained acceptability. William F. "Buffalo Bill" Cody was adamant that his exhibition was educational—a "place" and not a "show"—and continually reworked themes to keep up with historical events. At times, its Indian performers even played Chinese Boxers and Filipino rebels (Slotkin 1993:178). Performing in Buffalo Bill's Wild West provided needed income, an opportunity to travel, and also promoted interchanges and friendships among members of different tribal nations (most from the Northern Plains). As such, the exhibitions were one of the means of forming the modern concepts of intertribalism.

Audience demands of Wild West shows played an important part in the development of "fancy" war dances that had previously not existed in traditional Indian cultures. Although audiences found older war dances entertaining when a part of larger tableaux such as the Deadwood stage-coach raid reenactment, Cody, who later joined forces with Gordon "Pawnee Bill" Lillie, wanted more and asked male dancers to "fancy it up." That request resulted in the beginnings of modern Fancy Dance styles, in which dancing was done strictly for audience amusement. Grand entries, when dancers come into a pow-wow arena by category at the beginning of each session, are another Wild West show contribution, although one adapted from an earlier practice. Severt Young Bear recalls the function of the grand entry in a way that illustrates the cultural layering of warrior society, Wild West show, and contemporary pow-wow:

> A long time ago when there was any large gathering of dancers, they didn't do a grand entry like they do today at powwows where they come in to a special song after lining up outside the dance arena. They dance in lines and all dance in a circle till everybody has entered and forms a big circle in the center. I think this grand entry is based partly on some of the old warrior society parades but really is a result of Wild West shows and rodeos. Also, at dancing contests, which started in the 1960s, it allowed the committee to give points for coming in as part of the grand entry and to make sure all the dancers out there put on a good show for the audience. (Young Bear and Thiesz 1994:54)

Most Indian dancers and musicians in Buffalo Bill Cody's show were drawn from Lakota communities, and their musical culture responded by creating a new genre of song, the *Oskate Olowan*, which Willard Rhodes recorded during fieldwork on the Pine Ridge Reservation in 1939. Rhodes translated the genre's name as "Farewell Song for those leaving to join the circus."[6]

In spite of his strongly held views on Indian dances, Commissioner Burke was in attendance at the first large, intertribal, off-reservation pow-wow organized by Indians, which was held at the Haskell Institute in Lawrence, Kansas, in 1926. The message he sent by this action was clear: Dancing for the entertainment of a white audience was acceptable, dancing for the purpose of religion on the reservation was not.

What Burke failed to realize was that dancing could not be so easily separated from its older meanings in Indian life. More than likely, the dances he witnessed at Haskell had spiritual significance although he was unaware of it.

Government policies changed little during the Hoover administration, even though, technically, all Indians were now American citizens. "Because the Indians had failed at farming after the passage of the Dawes General Allotment Act, [Secretary of the Interior Ray Lyman] Wilbur stressed that their future lay in finding a place in the industrial life of the nation. He wanted educated Indians kept as far from their reservation as possible, while those who remained on the reservation should increase their contact with white neighbors" (Philip 1977:97).

The assimilationist philosophies of various missionary organizations continued to dominate BIA policies until the appointment of John Collier to the position of Indian commissioner in 1933. Collier had long been a crusader for Indian rights; in 1923 he was one of the founders of the Indian Defense Association. Although he possessed a somewhat romanticized view of Indian people and culture, his ideas about the importance of preserving Indian culture as a living tradition rather than a museum artifact marked a turning point in the bureau's policy. Not only did Collier legalize dancing for religious purposes, for example, but he also fostered it. "Collier encouraged the revival of ancient dances that had been previously frowned upon as heathenism. The Gros Ventres in North Dakota held ceremonies to petition the Great Spirit for prosperity; the Assiniboines performed a Rain Dance; and the Flathead, Blackfeet, and Crows made preparations for Sun Dances" (Philip 1977:184).

Legalizing religious dances also affected the principal purpose of pow-wows. No longer a spectacle for white entertainment, after World War II intertribal pow-wows grew out of community-serving veterans' homecoming celebrations. These events included parades, music, and dance and often had openly spiritual overtones. The element of entertainment remained, however, and by the mid-1950s the (initially) non-Indian concepts of competition and prize money had become increasingly important, ushering in the age of professional dancers who traveled a national circuit. In the North, pow-wows were more reservation-based because far more reservations existed there than in post–Dawes Act Oklahoma. For that reason, competition pow-wows took hold in the North slightly later than they did in the South. By the same token, however, Oklahoma people seem to hold more non-pow-wow, large-dance gatherings—such as Gourd Dances and Stomp Dances—than northerners, among whom pow-wows reign supreme.

The discussions that follow provide basic introductions to two primary cultural groups that will be discussed in the remainder of this text: the Lakota and the Anishnaabeg (fig. 1). For more in-depth information, I recommend *Standing in the Light: A Lakota Way of Seeing* by Severt Young Bear and R. D. Theisz (1994) and *The Ojibwe Dance Drum: Its History and Construction* by Thomas Vennum (1982).

The Lakota: People of the Pipe

Those who call themselves Lakota, a term that in their language means "allies," are members of a loosely organized confederation of seven Lakota-speaking tribal groups (known as Council Fires) now located in South and North Dakota. The Rendon family members profiled in chapter 5 are members of the Pine Ridge Oglala Lakota Nation, whose reservation is located in southwestern South Dakota. When considered as a cultural unit along with the Dakota and Nakota, the Lakota are part of the Great Sioux Nation that once stretched from central Minnesota though the Dakotas, Wyoming, and parts of Kansas and Colorado. The Sioux were the most powerful single political entity on the Northern Plains in the not-so-distant past and had enormous influence on the region's music and dance practices.

According to Lakota tradition, they originated as a people from Wind Cave in Paha Sapa (the Black Hills) of South Dakota, living first underground and then, as they emerged from the cave into the sunlight, follow-

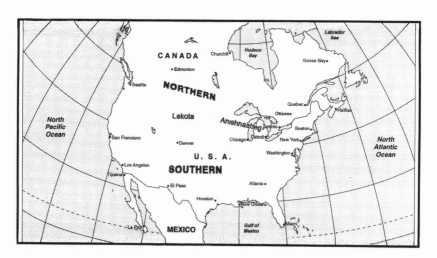

Figure 1. Pow-wow Styles and Tribal Areas

ing the buffalo. After centuries of life as a mobile people, moving from the Great Plains to the Eastern Woodlands and back again, they were visited by the White Buffalo Calf Woman, who presented them with a Sacred Pipe, a number of ceremonies, and songs to perform during these ceremonies. The pipe is now kept ("carried") by Arvol Looking-Horse, a member of the original family charged by White Buffalo Calf Woman with holding it.[7] In traditional Lakota religious life, the pipe is used for prayer, and the smoke serves as an offering to the spirits and Tunkashila (Grandfather). Because of the physical and spiritual geography of the land where they live—it is their origin place and where their creator gave them the central elements of their religions—the Lakota fought fiercely to protect it.

In the Lakota language, *waci* means the act of dancing, and *wacipi* defines the dance event. In earlier times, a wacipi could be held for any number of reasons, the most common of which was as a celebration of victory by a returning war or raiding party although dancing in some cases could be social as well. Religious dancing, specifically the Sun Dance, was for the most part unconnected to war dances. With the coming of the Omaha society, singers moved from playing individual hand drums while standing in a line to sitting around a big drum. Because of its warrior society roots, men were the primary active dancers to the sounds of the big drum; women stood around the periphery of the area, bobbing up and down to the beat. Dances in which women were more active were separate events, and male musicians reverted to hand drums when playing for them.

Between 1868, when the "Great Sioux Reservation" was established by treaty, and the massacre at Wounded Knee in 1890, the life of the Lakota was marked by conflict with the American government. When the Great Sioux Reservation was established, Congress recognized Lakota land holdings as encompassing approximately twenty million acres. In 1889, however, the reservation was split into five parts, and nine million acres (not including the Black Hills, which had been confiscated a decade before) were ceded and opened for non-Indian settlement (Densmore 1918:4). Further land was lost from the Pine Ridge Reservation during the late 1930s when the government "borrowed" the Badlands for use as a bombing range and then designated the area as a national park instead of returning it after World War II.

In 1882 the Sun Dance was outlawed at various agencies on the Great Sioux Reservation (Densmore 1918:86). The Lakota response was to take their ceremonies underground, often holding them in remote areas of reservations. Through this method, the Lakota retained much of their cultural knowledge of pre-reservation music and dance traditions. In the future, their growing population, combined with their reservation land-base, should protect them from being overwhelmed by outside musical influences. If anything, Lakota music and dance styles are arguably the largest single ingredient in the Northern pan-Indian pow-wow mix.

The Anishnaabeg: Fire and Music

The Anishnaabeg—People of the Three Fires Confederacy—are some of the earliest inhabitants of the American and Canadian Great Lakes region. The term *Anishnaabeg* loosely translates as "the people first put down by the Creator in this land." Their oral tradition tells of a great migration from the East hundreds of years ago, culminating in the settlement of large parts of Michigan, Wisconsin, and Minnesota. United in language and religion, three confederated tribes—the Ojibwe (the Older Brothers), Potawatomi (Bodewaadmi, the Fire Keepers), and Ottawa (Odawa, the Traders)—formed a strong alliance and were a potent political power in the Upper Midwest. Like most tribal groups in the United States, from the 1830s through the 1930s they suffered relocation and the loss of land to non-Indian encroachment. A surprising number of Anishnaabeg people, however, remain in the lands of their ancestors, practicing their traditional lifeways and spiritual beliefs.

The Anishnaabeg are one of the few eastern Indian nations to still occupy large tracts of land in the geographical area to which they hold aboriginal title. Ojibwe and Oji-Cree people can be found from central Ontario west through the Great Lakes, Minnesota, as far west as central Montana and as far north as southern Manitoba. As one of the most widespread Native cultural groups in North America, they are also one of the largest when populations on both sides of the border are counted. Of the Three Fires nations, the Ojibwe suffered the least dislocation with the arrival of the non-Native Canadians and Americans and were able to keep much of their pre-European culture intact to the present day. Both the Potawatomi and the Ottawa had some of their membership removed to Kansas and Oklahoma, where they remain as separate tribal entities from their Great Lakes counterparts.

Goverment officials who dealt with Woodlands Indians sanctioned two strategies. The first was removal to the West; the second was an imposition of Christianity coupled with the division of land belonging to bands (small groups of related families occupying the same geographic area) into individual allotments. Unalloted land was considered "unoccupied" and opened for white settlement. Of the Three Fires people, only the Ojibwe as a complete entity avoided removal west because they lived in areas less hospitable to agriculture. They did, however, lose al-

most all of their land. Under the Treaty of Detroit (1855), individual Great
Lakes Indians selected parcels of land of up to 160 acres to hold in pri-
vate ownership. Land they did not select was sold, creating a patchwork
of Indian and non-Indian property ownership. Often non-Indians were able
to steal remaining Indian land from its owners after its allotment, either
by forcibly driving the inhabitants away or by intricate legal subterfuge.
An example of the former took place in 1900, when the entire village of
Burt Lake, Michigan, was burned to the ground after local white residents
gained control of the property through tax fraud (Cornell 1986:101).

Many Anishnaabeg, especially those on Canadian reserves, still speak
their native language and participate in traditional religious observances
such as the ceremonies of the Midewiwin Lodge (the Anishnaabeg Grand
Medicine Society). In their worldview, religion and spirituality are not
separate from the business of daily life, and activities cannot necessarily
be conceptualized within the Western binary categories of sacred and secular. Therefore, traditional dance and music, even when performed at large,
competitive pow-wows and for a non-Indian audience, can still exist within
the realm of the spiritual or sacred. It often seems as if Indian participants
move in a reality set off from non-Indian observers, who tend to perceive
a pow-wow as a combination carnival and sporting event. These differing
sensibilities enable Indians to perform dances that, although in a commercial setting, have profound spiritual meaning for them.

Anishnaabeg pow-wow dancing has a different genealogy than that
performed on the Great Plains. As documented by Thomas Vennum
(1980, 1982), there were strong Plains influences in the late 1800s: contact with the Dakota Omaha society and the Ojibwe oral tradition of
receiving the big drum sometime during the 1870s from a Sioux known
as Tailfeather Woman. According to Vennum:

> The salient themes in Tailfeather Woman's story remain constant in the
> many versions collected. A Sioux woman, who fled United States sol-
> diers who were killing her people, hid in a lake for four days. During this
> time, she was visited by the Great Spirit who instructed her to make a
> large dance drum and taught her the songs and (presumably) ritual de-
> tails for their use. The Drum was built as an instrument of peace and
> was meant to be copied and passed on to other tribes to bring an end to
> bloodshed. (1982:45)

Even though the Western Ojibwe had continual contact with the
Dakota and their warrior society traditions, the story of Tailfeather Woman and her drum—also the basis for stories of the pow-wow drum tradition as told by most contemporary Anishnaabeg—imparts distinctive
meaning to their music, divergent from that of the Plains Indians. An-

ishnaabeg dancing and music is closely connected with a Drum exchange ceremony that establishes peaceful relationships among tribal people and villages. Lakota dancing, however, is a direct outgrowth of old warrior society celebrations. Throw into this mix the age-old musical practices of the Midewiwin along with the intertribal cross-fertilization of Wild West shows and the dance exhibition circuit, and, on the surface, the result covers deep structural differences in purpose and meaning.

The Ann Arbor Pow-wow: A Brief Case Study

In 1989, while conducting fieldwork for a project that ultimately did not result in a filed master's thesis, I assembled a musical ethnography of the Ann Arbor, Michigan, pow-wow, at the time the largest event of its kind in the state. Since then I have danced at Ann Arbor every year, been a member of the pow-wow committee, and worked in various roles, from security and finances (counting money as it came in) to registering dancers. My project in 1989 enabled me to gather historical information on the roots of the pow-wow, and my participation in years following has allowed me to see the event grow and change. Reflecting these experiences, the information that follows is meant to provide an overview of how one small, community-based gathering has grown into a major event. Although it would be helpful to declare this particular pow-wow as representative of most events, that statement would be deceptive because pow-wows are so varied. Nevertheless, I know the Dance at Ann Arbor better than any other (except, perhaps, the UCLA Pow-wow, which is predominantly Southern) and can discuss it in the most detail.

The Ann Arbor Pow-wow, part of both the larger complex of Northern pow-wow events and traditions, is representative of a typical Anishnaabeg-dominated event. Within these two larger frameworks, it is also the product of a unique set of circumstances, including (within the Detroit area) the influence of non-Anishnaabeg Indian cultures and the pressures placed upon a community-based event by a large university that intends to portray itself as supporting the Native American community. In more than a quarter-century of existence the pow-wow has changed from a small, traditional affair into a competitive extravaganza complete with concerts, affiliated "dry dances," and raffles.[8]

In Michigan, the earliest pow-wow–like events preexist the area's incorporation into the United States and have been described by Gertrude Kurath in *Michigan Indian Festivals* (1966). Under the heading "Ceremonies of the Cycle," Kurath summarizes the proceedings at such a ceremony:

A ceremony could involve an individual, a family, a clan, a tribe or several tribes; men only, women only, or all ages and sexes. The typical procedure of a ceremonial gathering was as follows:

1. Preliminaries, with invitations by messengers who carried prayer sticks; food collection; in sugar making camps, begging processions by masked children.
2. Offerings in the central home or on the dance place, depending on the season—a tobacco invocation; offerings of food and clothing; perhaps a dog sacrifice.
3. Prayers and speeches by sponsors, shamans and chiefs.
4. Songs by special singers with drums; dancing by the assembly or by expert soloists; sometimes social dances all night long.
5. Feasting on regional foods.

The tobacco offerings, which opened the ceremonies, could take place in the form of sprinkling on the central fire (Sacred Fire) or smoking a pipe which made the rounds. In peace parleys it was a dance of one or two male experts. Calendric Offerings would follow the course of the sun, from east to north, to each cardinal direction in turn. Then they addressed the sky and the earth. Theoretically all should have four repeats. The number four also determined the number of festive days. (1966:15)

"Though the native ceremonies have vanished in Michigan," she adds (21), "fragments remain as single dances and songs, along with memories of the uses and beliefs. The vestiges are but dim echoes of the aboriginal forms. Rather, they were echoes. By 1966 most genuine survivals had vanished, along with the traditionalists who recalled them." Any number of Anishnaabeg would strongly disagree with that point. Traditional religion went underground, as it did on the Great Plains, due to government persecution of its adherents.

Although it is unclear which period Kurath is describing—it could be pre-1700 or pre-1900—her outline of ceremonies resembles accounts of gatherings referred to as "camp meetings." In addition to dancing, these events also had feasting and spiritual gatherings. "Camp meeting" is also a term used for large, multi-day Christian Revival convocations and was probably borrowed from Euro-American usage at the turn of the nineteenth century. Many older members of the southeastern Michigan Anishnaabeg community consider camp meetings to be the true precursors of their local pow-wows. There is, however, one major difference: None of my consultants suggested that a camp meeting was (or is) an intertribal event in the way of a pow-wow. Indian camp meetings were usually held on or near reservations, and there is no indication that non-tribal members were welcome. That restriction likely was not as true for Christian camp meetings.

The earliest camp meetings that those whom I interviewed recalled were in the mid-1940s; the earliest Ann Arbor–area pow-wow was at Carleton Fields in the mid-1950s. All consultants agreed that competition pow-wows began in the state sometime between 1968 and 1972, probably in the Detroit area. Other now-prominent Michigan pow-wows began during the late 1960s in Lansing, Kalamazoo, Detroit, and Mount Pleasant, all the locales of universities. Michigan State University is in Lansing, Western Michigan in Kalamazoo, Wayne State in Detroit, and Central Michigan in Mount Pleasant. Each of the pow-wows are held at the universities, although the Lansing Indian community holds a separate, traditional event as well.

Few written records on the Ann Arbor Pow-wow existed until the 1980s. Because of the turnover of personnel within the university's Office of Minority Student Services, early records relating to the event cannot be located. For Indian people, however, specific dates and figures are not as important as the overall flow of events, and those with whom I spoke reflected such priorities. Because of that sensibility, most pre-1985 narrative contains few specific dates but is made up of interwoven, sometimes conflicting, accounts of the pow-wow from three very different vantage points: the university's, Irving "Hap" McCue's, and Mike Dashner's.

The official University of Michigan version of the Ann Arbor Pow-wow is not lengthy:

> The Ann Arbor Pow Wow has its origin in the Indian community in and around Ann Arbor. The first was held in 1972 out in the open, west of town. From year to year the Pow Wow flourished as its site alternated among Huron High School, the Women's League, Michigan Union, Cleary College, and the Coliseum. With the formation of N.A.S.A. (Native American Students Association) in 1976, Native American students made the Pow-Wow a focus of their interest and enthusiasm. Today, the gathering remains a university and community celebration with the participation constantly growing. (Ann Arbor Pow-wow program, April 12, 1986)

The genesis of the contemporary Ann Arbor Pow-wow lay in the coming together of members of the Ann Arbor Native American community and members of the Title IV Program staff (part of the Indian Education Act) in 1972. Community members desired to have an event that would give area public school students an opportunity to feel pride in their Indian heritage. At the same time, they sought a positive way to present Native culture to Ann Arbor and Washtenaw County. The first local pow-wow was held at Mexicanas Hall near Dexter in the spring of 1972. Three Drums were present: the Blue Lake Drum of Jose Marcus,

Teofilo Lucero's Drum from Detroit, and a Drum based at Wayne State University and run by Bob Thomas. Lucero and Marcus are both originally from Taos, New Mexico, and Thomas is Cherokee. Although a number of Anishnaabeg men sat in with both Drums as guests, there were no Anishnaabeg Drums in the Ann Arbor or Detroit areas at the time.

All three Drums sang in the Northern Plains style, even though all three head singers were from areas geographically in the realm of the Southern style of singing. Lucero and Marcus picked up that manner of singing while they traveled around the Northern Plains; it is unclear where, or how, Thomas learned to sing in the Northern Plains style. Both Lucero and Marcus are influential musicians in the greater Detroit area, Marcus because of his fine singing voice and Lucero because of his vast repertoire of songs. The Marcus and the Lucero families are mentioned in Kurath's text (1966:60).

In the years following its 1972 inauguration, the pow-wow moved among four different locations. It was in Ypsilanti for two years, at Huron High School for three, at Pioneer High School for one, and twice at Ypsilanti's Cleary College.The group that ran the pow-wow referred to itself as the "American Indian Culture School," the *Ann Arbor News* noted on March 8, 1976. At first, prize money was small, just enough to pay a dancer's expenses. Large "feeds" were staged for not only the dancers and Drums but also the Indian community as a whole. Hap McCue, one of the event's founders, recalls that one year forty turkeys were cooked and more than two hundred potatoes were peeled.

During this same period, the first professional dancers began to show up at the pow-wow, and they expected more prize money than the amounts being offered. In order to attract them regularly, more substantial funding had to be found. The pow-wow had become unable to sustain itself by gate money and fees from traders alone. At one event in the late 1970s, community members used money from their own pockets to create a large enough pot. In 1982—in order to survive—the pow-wow was brought under the financial umbrella of the University of Michigan.

The individual who was primarily responsible for the move was Moose Pamp, the Native American representative in the Office of Minority Student Services. Moose has died, but his mother, Betty Pamp, described his role in the evolution of the Ann Arbor Pow-wow. The original group that had sponsored the event had lost cohesion. Hap McCue had temporarily departed, and Teofilo Lucero was aging. It seemed logical for the University Native American Student Association (NASA) to take charge of the event.

The union marked the beginning of an ongoing partnership between the Ann Arbor Indian community and the university's Indian students. The students, who were from throughout the country, gained ties with the local Indian community and in the process learned management and leadership skills needed to organize a major event every spring. The Indian community benefited from having its pow-wow stabilized, therefore bringing in more dancers, Drums, and traders. Because one of the primary purposes of a pow-wow is to bring Indian people together, an event's success is gauged by how many attend.

The University of Michigan, however, had its own agenda for the pow-wow, and at times that diverged markedly from the Indian community's. As a tool for creating a better public image, the university sought to make the pow-wow as large as possible. After five years of growth under Moose Pamp, a full-time administrator for the event was hired and, like Pamp, given the title of Native American representative in the Office for Minority Student Services. That individual, Mike Dashner, was a former Michigan student and a well-known competitive pow-wow dancer. With his hiring, the region's Indian community lost control of its pow-wow, and the Native American Student Association become sponsors in name only. For the next seven years, Indian students had little say about how the event was operated. They had become primarily unpaid labor at their own event.

In the meantime, the pow-wow's expansion did serve the needs of Native American professional dancers and "pow-wow families," literally entire families who travel as groups to all major pow-wows in a particular geographic area in order to support themselves by winning prize money. Some members of a family dance, some sit at a Drum (many do both), and others set up a booth and trade. As families of professional pow-wow dancers began to dominate the event, smaller, local traders were often overwhelmed and local dancers placed less and less often in the competitions. As the decade came to a close, the pow-wow had become more and more oriented toward being a public relations forum for the university. University president James Duderstadt, for example, opened the event in 1989 with a welcoming address. The next morning, a color photograph of him speaking to the assembly appeared on the front page of the *Ann Arbor News.*

The effects of Dashner's hiring and the university's takeover were not entirely negative, however. Dashner's connections on the larger pow-wow circuit enabled him to bring in big-name Drums, and his fund-raising savvy yielded greater support from the university and the Ann Arbor–area business community. The result was a bigger and better (as measured by dancer and audience head-counts) pow-wow each year. By the early 1990s,

1. Omaha dancers on the Pine Ridge, S.D., Reservation, 1902. Bell Studios photograph, author's collection.

2. A Grass dancer at the Sault Ste. Marie, Mich., Traditional Pow-wow, July 1995. Photograph by the author.

3. A male Fancy dancer at the University of California, Los Angeles Pow-wow, May 1998. The eagle feathers in his roach are set in a "rocker," Southern-style. The Drum (Southern Thunder, Pawnee) is in the background. Southern Drums set up in the center of a dance arena, a location Anishnaabeg Drums also prefer. Photograph by the author.

4. Teenage male Northern Traditional and Southern Straight dancers line up for judging at the 1998 UCLA Pow-wow. Photograph by the author.

5. Women's Fancy dancers enter the arena in preparation for competition at the 1998 Eastern Michigan University, Ypsilanti, Pow-wow. Photograph by the author.

6. Women's Fancy dancers in competition at the Eastern Michigan University Pow-wow, September 1998. The Drums are all located at the side of the arena. During indoor pow-wows, Drums are usually arranged along the outer edge of an arena. Photograph by the author.

7. A trader's stand at the Eastern Michigan University Pow-wow, 1988. The trader, Delores Fisher from Walpole Island, Canada, can be found at most pow-wows in southeastern Michigan. Her crafts are all homemade, and the sweet grass she sells is freshly picked and braided. Photograph by the author.

8. Susan Hill (Mohawk), left, in Jingle Dance regalia and Laura Koda (Odawa) get ready to set up camp at the Sault Ste. Marie, Mich., Traditional Pow-wow, July 1995. Photograph by the author.

9. Susan Hill (Mohawk), left, and Evelyn George (Seneca) at the Ann Arbor Pow-wow, 1999. George wears an Iroquoian-style women's Traditional outfit. The men's version of this regalia has begun to be placed in its own competition category, "men's Eastern Straight," at some pow-wows. If contesting at a Southern pow-wow she would be able to compete in the women's Cloth category, but at Northern events she must compete with dancers in fully beaded Northern Plains–style buckskin dresses. Photograph by the author.

10. Frances Densmore plays a recording for Mountain Chief (Blackfoot) at the Smithsonian Institution, 1916. Harris and Ewing Photographers, author's collection.

11. A Drum group, including an outer circle of female singers, at the Pendleton, Ore., Round Up, 1911. Mancell Studios photograph, author's collection.

12. The Porcupine Singers (Oglala Lakota), UCLA Pow-wow, 1998. Photograph by the author.

13. During breaks at the 1998 UCLA Pow-wow, the Porcupine Singers carefully covered their drum. Photograph by the author.

14. Drum groups at the University of Michigan, Flint, Traditional Pow-wow, 1997. Even though this is an indoor event, Drums have been located the center of the arena. Directly behind the Canadian flag are the Blue Lake Singers of Ypsilanti, a regionally respected Drum. Founded by José Marcus (Taos Pueblo) in the 1970s, the Blue Lake Singers are proficient in both the Northern and Southern styles. Photograph by the author.

Drums participated by invitation only, and major groups such as Whitefish Bay, Blackfoot Crossing, and Blacklodge were accepting invitations. The Southern tradition was not well represented, however. Only Winnebago/Ho-Chunk Drums such as Bear Clan from the Milwaukee area and Wisconsin Dells from central Wisconsin attended, although at times Dashner did invite Iroquoian Drums, many of whom sing in the Southern style.

Inside the 1989 Ann Arbor Pow-wow

Planning for the 1989 Ann Arbor Pow-wow began in September 1988 as Mike Dashner selected an appropriate weekend in March. The date was chosen because of two considerations: availability of space in an appropriate campus arena and what proved to be an unsuccessful attempt to avoid a scheduling conflict with the March Pow-wow in Denver, the first major event of the pow-wow season (which runs from March to November). The Denver March Pow-wow in 1989 was nearly four times the size of the Ann Arbor event, with prize money and prestige proportionately greater as well. Such conflicts made getting a "name" Drum difficult for the smaller event and also made it harder to attract the better dancers on the circuit. The weekend of March 18 and 19 was selected because, by tradition, the Denver event was held on the second weekend of that month. Unfortunately for Ann Arbor, Denver moved its date up by a week that year, which created a conflict.

The next step in the planning process was to form committees within the Native American Student Association to manage specific aspects of the pow-wow. The committees were for publicity, fund-raising, advertising, the program, food, clean-up, and the giveaway. All work to be done by student committees (except the giveaway) would be supervised so closely by Dashner that the students would, in effect, lose their autonomy. Jim Beck, a university employee who claims Ojibwe ancestry, was also heavily involved in the pow-wow that year, especially in accounting for funds generated by gate revenues. In addition, NASA members volunteered for such duties as collecting admission money, selling tickets for the fundraising raffle, and providing security. Because of a lack of student volunteers, non-Native community members assisted with security, registering Drums and dancers, and keeping track of admission money. Many of the non-Natives were from the University of Michigan's Baha'i organization. Members of the Michigamua fraternity also volunteered to work but were rejected because of NASA's ongoing conflict with them over Michigamua's use of pseudo-Indian rituals in initiation ceremonies.

Although it caused many student complaints, Dashner's control over so many facets of pow-wow planning undoubtedly was the reason for the event's expansion under his authority. To be fair, the university's administration considered the pow-wow to be part of his job, and he had final responsibility for its financial outcome. Dashner's connections within the Michigan bureaucracy, combined with his knowledge of the pow-wow circuit, enabled him to raise funds to contact a headline group, the Rocky Boy Singers, an Ojibwe-Cree Drum from Rocky Boy, Montana, and persuade them to play in Ann Arbor rather than at the Denver event. The 1989 pow-wow was the first in Ann Arbor to have a well-known western Drum in attendance, something Dashner had sought since he took control of the event. Although the Rocky Boy singers had been in Denver the previous weekend to play at the wake of Nadine (Little-Sky) Rendon, the group had flown on to Ann Arbor instead of remaining in Denver.[9] What they would earn by performing at Ann Arbor was likely the equivalent of the amount awarded to a group that wins a Drum competition, about $2,500 plus travel expenses. Because there was no guarantee of a win at Denver, coming to Ann Arbor was a solid financial move.

In addition to the Rocky Boy Singers, six Drums were officially invited to the pow-wow: the All Nation Singers (Illinois), Baraga Singers (Michigan), Bear Clan Singers (Wisconsin), Smokey Town (Wisconsin), Three Fires (Minnesota), and White Eye Singers (Canada). With the exception of Bear Clan (Winnebago) and Smokey Town (Menominee), all Drums were Anishnaabeg. The host Drum, the All Nation Singers, had at one time included Mike Dashner as a member. A number of Drums also had important political connections. The Bear Clan Singers are members of the Cleveland family, and Three Fires is the Drum of Eddie Benton-Benai, at the time keeper of the Western Door for the Midewiwin. As invited drums, the groups were assured of receiving a minimum payment. By tradition, one host Drum should be from the immediate geographical area of a pow-wow, as was the Blue Lake Drum of Ypsilanti. Blue Lake, Jose Marcus's Drum, is politically unimportant, however, and was not officially invited.

Dashner had decided that the head dancers should be recently graduated students of the University of Michigan, in keeping with the pow-wow's theme, "Excellence and Tradition." Influential members of the Native community were selected as head veterans and judges, and the master of ceremonies was a friend of Dashner. Nepotism and the dispensing of favors for relatives and friends is a common and often acceptable practice in most Native American cultures, and those in positions of authority are expected to do so. The practice is handled in the same manner in the dominant society. The greatest contrast between the two groups, however, is in the openness of the nepotism and the openness of complaining about it.

The major source of contention that year was Dashner's plan to present President Duderstadt with a handmade commemorative knife. Members of American Indians at the University of Michigan (AIUM)—a faculty, staff, and graduate student organization—strongly objected. Customarily, when a person is given a knife as a gift they are expected to give a round object of some kind in return. To inform a non-Indian of the custom was regarded as offensive by some, and others thought that giving a knife without the expectation of receiving a round object in return constituted an act of hostility toward Duderstadt. A compromise was found. Duderstadt was to be told that he should give a penny in return for the knife but not the reason for doing so. The decision took two hours of often rancorous debate, which made me wonder if the issue was a proxy for other, deeper problems.

The Pow-wow in Action

In 1989, news of the date of the Ann Arbor Pow-wow traveled through the pow-wow circuit primarily by word of mouth and also through advertisements in Indian newspapers such as *News from Indian Country*. Posters were put up in Ann Arbor, and flyers were handed out at other pow-wows (fig. 2). In spite of the local advertising, the majority of the singers and dancers came from outside southeastern Michigan. The Ann Arbor event had been established long enough that people were aware of its approximate time of year. Because it was a university-sponsored event, the prize money advertised was sure to be paid, which gave Ann Arbor priority over other midwestern pow-wows happening the same weekend. Unpaid prize money in the form of paper IOUs had been a problem in the Midwest and Great Lakes regions during the late 1980s, and dancers had little recourse other than to vote with their feet and not attend that event the following year.

On Saturday, March 18, the traders were the first to arrive at the Coliseum on Hill Street. They set up tables inside in a large circle surrounding the dance arena. Dancers and Drums started drifting in about 10 A.M., signing in at registration tables before setting up or beginning to dress in regalia. In addition to the six Drums officially invited, other groups were registered to perform: Wasenoday, and the White Eye Singers, Eagle Feather Singers, Keweenaw Bay Singers, Two Hawk Singers, Red Eagle Singers, Young Nation Singers, Wisconsin Dell Singers, Blue Lake

The University of Michigan's 27th Annual

ANN ARBOR POW WOW

"Dance for Mother Earth"

MARCH 26, 27 & 28, 1999
U-M CRISLER ARENA

A Native American song and dance celebration featuring over 1,000 of North America's greatest champion singers and dancers. Come see the rich culture and heritage of the country's most renowned Native American craftspeople and artists displaying and selling their authentic work.

DOORS OPEN FRIDAY 5:00 pm
Friday Grand Entry 7:00 pm
with singing & dancing until 11:00 pm
DOORS OPEN SATURDAY 11:00 am
Saturday Grand Entries 1:00 pm & 7:00 pm
with singing & dancing until 11:00 pm
DOORS OPEN SUNDAY 11:00 am
Sunday Grand Entry 1:00 pm
with the Pow Wow concluding at 6:00 pm

Adults $8/day
Senior citizens $6/day
College students (with valid ID) $6/day
Students (13-17 yrs.) $6/day
Children (4-12 yrs.) $4/day
3 yrs. & under FREE
Weekend Passes available
ALL TICKETS ON SALE AT THE DOOR
Handicap Entrance on west side of arena

PUBLIC WELCOME TO ALL EVENTS
JOIN US AND SHARE THE EXPERIENCE!

For more information call the Pow Wow Infoline at (734) 64-POW99 or Shannon Martin at (734) 763-9044
Visit the Ann Arbor Pow Wow web site: http://www.umich.edu/~powwow

THIS IS AN ALCOHOL AND SUBSTANCE FREE EVENT

Hosted by the Native American Student Association and the Office of Multi-Ethnic Student Affairs a Division of Student Affairs

Figure 2. Ann Arbor Pow-wow Flyer

Singers, and Sweetgrass Singers. Of the non-invited Drums, three were not Anishnaabeg: the Young Nation Singers (Tonawanda Mohawk Reserve), the Blue Lake Singers (Taos Pueblo/intertribal), and Wisconsin Dells (Winnebago). The Baraga Singers, although invited, did not attend.

From copies of dancer and Drum registration forms I have been able to delineate certain trends and preferences by tribal nation and age groupings within each larger dance type. Men's Traditional dancing, for example, is most popular among the Anishnaabeg, Northern Plains Nations, and tribes such as the Winnebago from Central and Eastern Woodlands culture areas. For them, Traditional dance styles and the regalia of the pow-wow can be traced directly to pre-reservation forms. This mode of performance, however, is not part of Iroquoian culture, whose nations have their own distinctive regalia and dance styles although both female and male Iroquoian sometimes dance in Plains outfits. When Iroquois dancers do contest in "Indian clothes," they rarely win (except in the Smoke Dance) when they wear them outside the Northeast. Dances of more recent origin, however, such as the Fancy styles—especially the Jingle Dress Dance—are fast gaining adherents in Six Nations communities, and pow-wows are beginning to be considered *Ongwehonwe* (Real People) events rather than dance exhibitions.

The year 1989 marked the final time the Ann Arbor Pow-wow was held in the Hill Street Coliseum. The following year, it moved to Crisler Arena (the basketball court) and promptly doubled in size. By 1992 more than four hundred dancers were attending, and Drums were by invitation only. In a bid to further increase revenues, the pow-wow became a three-day (Friday, Saturday, and Sunday) event in 1994. That year also marked the last with Mike Dashner in charge. For reasons still unclear, he received a "lateral transfer" to another university position and by 1997 had left the campus altogether. Shannon Martin (Ojibwe), a recent graduate of the School of Engineering, was hired as a one-year replacement and in 1996 became permanent. Her tenure was marked by fundamental changes in pow-wow operation, including a genuine, student-run committee system and widening the event's base by inviting Southern/Oklahoma Drums and quality local Drums such as the Blue Lake Singers. Martin in many ways returned the pow-wow to the greater Indian community and at times took stands counter to university policies and aims.

In the spring of 2000, the Indian student organization and a multiracial campus alliance, the Students of Color Coalition (SCC), clashed once again with the Michigamua fraternity, which is affiliated with the school's athletic programs. From February 6 until March 13, protesters occupied Michigamua's offices (the Michigamua "wigwam") in the Michigan

Union building. The university received nationwide negative publicity from January through the summer months, in large part because, as a passive form of endorsement, the University of Michigan had been allowing office space to the fraternity, without charge, for more than seventy-five years. Shannon Martin spent many days working on pow-wow preparation during her regular office hours and then spent evenings as a liaison between the SCC and the administration, in the process earning large amounts of compensatory overtime.

Her actions also created a direct link between the pow-wow and the protesters, a point Michigamua members and alumni took note of. In retaliation for the Native student and community protest, Michigamua's allies in student government blocked any more than token funding for the pow-wow. Rent for Crisler Arena, controlled by the university's athletic programs, suddenly jumped to $6,000 per day, which caused a serious financial crisis for the event's planners.

With careful financial planning, however, the Ann Arbor Pow-wow went forward, but for the first time in its history as a politicized event. Speakers denounced Michigamua and their perceptions of the university's inaction; a protest march was held after the Friday dance session, with marchers converging on university president Lee Bollinger's home.

On March 15, two days after the end of the SCC Michigan Union occupation and just a week before the pow-wow, Royster Harper, Michigan's vice president for student affairs, appointed a faculty and student panel to consider the university's policies on issues of space allocation and student groups. On April 24 the panel issued nine recommendations, one of which was that all organizations using university space be "made aware of the importance of respectful engagement with diverse perspectives. In particular," the panel urged, "those groups using University space [should] avoid the perpetuation of degrading group caricatures. Names, rituals, and symbolism that caricature minority groups foster distrust, undermine community and present a false picture of University values" (Seguine 2000).

Bollinger did not respond to the committee's recommendations until August 14, when in a letter to Michigamua, Phoenix, and Vulcan (the latter two being sororities associated with Michigamua) he wrote, "Consistent with the principles of fairness and access expressed in the panel's recommendations, I have decided that it is not appropriate to continue any special tenancy in the [Michigan Union] tower space for Michigamua, Phoenix and Vulcan." There would be a transitional period, and then, "If they choose to apply for office and meeting space after this transitional period, they will do so as part of the general process of student space allocation" (Peterson 2000). During the summer months, Martin's supervisors ordered her to use the compensatory overtime she had accumulated. She did so by repatriating to various Michigan tribes objects such as pipes and a traditional cradleboard that SCC members had found in the Michigamua wigwam during the takeover (something Michigamua had agreed to do).

How events of the spring and summer of 2000 will resonate through future Ann Arbor Pow-wows is open to question. With the university's loss of control over the publicity generated by Native students, and the sometimes adversarial stance of its own employees, Michigan may no longer want to continue with the pow-wow under its funding umbrella. Although pow-wows in general are rarely politically charged events, bringing a community-based dance into a political university forum was, in retrospect, an invitation for the academy's most cherished possession—freedom of speech—to be applied liberally by its Native students, alumni, staff, and faculty.

3 Dance Styles and Regalia

At Northern pow-wows, dancers in specific categories are set apart as being eligible to compete for prize money. In addition, there are two other broad categories: "specials" and open intertribal dances. Of these categories, open intertribal dancing does not have particularly distinctive footwork, nor does it have regalia requirements other than the custom of women wearing shawls over their shoulders (although that is not required). Special dances are held outside the contest rounds and intertribal rounds and include Hoop dancing, Aztec dancing, and other tribal-specific exhibitions such as Inuit or Northwest Coast styles. Memorials and honorings of various kinds are also classified as specials (chapter 5). In this chapter I will concentrate on the evolution of contest styles, specifically on the four major dances commonly used in Northern competition: men's and women's Traditional, men's and women's Fancy (or women's Fancy Shawl), the Grass Dance (men only), and the Jingle Dress Dance (women only). To some extent, the footwork of these dances is determined by the music that accompanies them—the drum's pulsation pattern and tempo or both. More than anything else, internal standards— unconscious theories—and externally imposed conventions in the form of judging norms are what drive fashions in dance footwork and regalia.

Footwork is the same at the most basic levels of competitive and intertribal dancing. For men, each foot alternates in extending forward and tapping twice, more lightly on the first drumbeat. The dancer's weight shifts forward onto the foot for the second step. The legs alternate as the body moves forward. According to one tradition, the step honors the "four-leggeds" (various mammals) that taught Indians how to dance by imitating an animal's four-legged gait. Each human leg makes two motions to represent legs on each side of an animal's body. Another belief is that the ability to dance—to pray using motion—is a gift to Natives from the Creator. Women's basic intertribal footwork is closer to a stylized walk, with each leg taking a full step every two drumbeats. Women have the choice, however, of using the same intertribal step as men, and often they do.

A number of factors determine the look of an individual's dance regalia. Each type of contest dancing has a preexisting template for regalia, largely determined by custom. Because of that, most dancers' decisions about large-scale regalia are automatic once the dancers choose a dance type. For example, women's Traditional dancers must wear a dress or shirt and skirt combination that reaches at least a few inches below the knees; they should also drape a shawl over their left arm and carry a fan in their right hand. Other regalia items—purse, breastplate, scarf, belt, and jewelry—are determined by personal choice, as are colors and fabrics. Outfits can be simple or spectacular, depending on financial resources. Some people purchase complete outfits, and others make theirs from scratch. The average dancer wears a mixture of homemade, inherited, gifted, and purchased regalia. A good set often takes years to assemble, and dancers are always on the lookout at pow-wow traders' booths for something special in "their" colors.

Traditional Dances

What are now known as the men's and women's Traditional and men's Fancy Dance styles are directly descended from earlier, pre-reservation-era forms. Traditional dances have roots in old, tribal-specific warrior societies, old Omaha/Grass styles, and, to a certain extent, the Oklahoma Dream Dance of the 1890s that spread into the Great Lakes region. With so many variables, there is no one definitive Traditional Dance. Each dancer presents a slightly different version, depending on tribal affiliation and personal preference. Competition judging also has a personalized element, with no absolute standards.

Women's Traditional dancing can be characterized as having two basic footwork forms: moving forward step by step or standing in one spot, feet together, and using the knees and balls of the feet to bob up and down while keeping the upper body erect. The former is common to the Great Lakes and Oklahoma regions and the latter to the Northern Plains. In either case, by tradition a woman's feet should never completely leave the ground, which symbolizes the close bonds between women and their

Mother the Earth. Most important, while her feet are on the ground the fringe on a woman's outfit should be in motion, swinging in wide arcs.

Before World War I, Plains women rarely entered dance grounds other than during specific women's dances, which tended to be what are referred to as "side-steps" (now often a Traditional women's competition dance). Most of the time, girls and women danced around the edges, either standing in place or moving slowly. That custom began to change following World War I and accelerated after World War II and the advent of large-scale homecoming celebrations, in part because women had served in the Armed Forces in large numbers. In many ways, the privilege of dancing in the interior of an arena was as much associated with a veteran's status as it was gender.

As more women became veterans, more roles—such as flag-bearer—became open to them. Before the late nineteenth century, Great Lakes–area women, to a certain extent, danced at ceremonial grounds during the same time men did and in addition had special *kwe* (women's) dances. After the introduction of the Dream Dance Society by Tailfeather Woman, however, Anishnaabeg women's roles changed to support male singers and dancers (similar to the Great Plains ideal). Women did little dancing within the arena until after World War II.

Women's Traditional regalia has more variety than that of any other women's dance style, in large part because it can either be in the Plains fashion (buckskin) or taken from old-time (1840–1900) fancy-dress clothes "traditional" to the dancer's tribe. In reality, the style that almost always wins in competition is that of Northern Buckskin dancers, who wear fully beaded yokes with long fringe, deer or cowhide skirts, women's breastplate (with vertically oriented bone pipes), leggings, moccasins, a fan in their right hands, and a shawl draped over their left arms (photograph 18). Women's Northern Cloth regalia styles are far more varied and include the ribbonwork/applique dresses of the Great Lakes and Iroquoian Cloth Dance dresses (photograph 9). Strangely enough, many women who dance in the Northern Buckskin Dance also use forward-motion footwork, although it is inappropriate to the dress. Conversely, local judges ignorant of the proper footwork for the Buckskin style often penalize women from the Northern Plains for not moving when those women dance outside their region. Too often, competitions are won by women who have impressive regalia but inappropriate footwork.

Men's Traditional Dance footwork is more free-form than women's, and men's regalia is more complex. Several factors affect what a man wears: tribal origin, personal sensibility, inheritance of dance accessories, and how well his wife, mother, or partner can sew. Traditional dancers move forward slowly, sometimes zigzagging while stomping their feet. Bowing and moving the head and body in sudden, jerking motions reminiscent of the head motions of animals are often favored. In this dance, men tell a story, sometimes of war and valor and other times of hunting and animal-spirit possession. Each story is personal, and a good dancer conveys the excitement of his dance narrative to the audience. Male Northern Traditional dancers, in addition to whatever personal regalia they possess, such as eagle feathers, a breastplate with horizontally oriented bone pipes, a roach, and a fan, are almost always marked by a single back bustle, two cloth trailers hanging from it. Although traditional warrior society dancers wore very little body covering and danced with bare chests and legs, modern dancers almost always wear full shirts and leggings, reminiscent of the dance clothing worn only in the winter months of the late 1800s. The male Traditional dancer in photograph 20 wears "contemporary Traditional" regalia; the outfit in photograph 22 is an example of "old-style Northern Traditional." At larger pow-wows, these two sub-styles now compete in separate categories.

For both men and women, "Traditional" is also a catchall category, and regalia styles not considered Fancy, Grass, or Jingle Dress are thrown into it by default. In practical terms, that can mean anything from Southeastern (Choctaw/Cherokee) women's Cloth Dance dresses to hobbyists (non-Indian dancers) who wear clothing inspired by the *Lord of the Rings* trilogy. During my years of pow-wow dancing I have never seen anyone who has paid the registration fee be excluded from a competition, even when they wear almost nothing—which was the case when two men brought only one outfit between them and split its parts.

The Contemporary Grass Dance

Peji Waci is the traditional name Lakota people use for the Grass Dance, which is popular at modern intertribal pow-wows in the United States and Canada. Contemporary Lakota dancers tell their own tale of Grass Dance origins, very much different from most written accounts. Norma Rendon's (Oglala) narrative, which she first heard from her grandfather, Wallace Little, is representative:

> The Grass Dance originated way back. The Lakota, a long time ago they had these men who would wear a row of grass around their head, around their arms, around their ankles, and right under their knees. And the reason for this is they would always be in front. Before they would go to a battle or a hunt, these men would always be up front. And they would creep down in with the grass and blend right in with the grass. They

would sneak up on the buffalo or the camp they were going to attack. They went up front because they blended right in with the grass when they were sneaking up. Then, when the hunt was over or the war was over, the war party ended, then they came back to camp and were the first ones to dance. They were also the first ones to go into the dance. As they went into the dance arena before the People they would stomp down the grass with their feet. And that's why when you see Grass dancers they're stomping their feet all four ways. If they do a movement four times on one side, then they do that movement four times on the other side. If you watch Grass dancers now they still do that. (August 15, 1989, interview)

Rendon's account is consistent with both the contemporary dance's footwork and the look of its regalia. The most characteristic element of Grass Dance footwork—"flattening the grass"—entails partially bending on one leg while dragging the foot of the other leg out and around the body and tapping the ball of each foot four times. Grass dancers' outfits have no feather bustles but do include large amounts of chainette fringe or yarn, which is attached to their shirts and aprons and, when moving, evokes waves of grass. Dancers also wear a roach and carry fans in their left hands. Various objects can be carried in their right hands, including dream-catchers, mirrors, and small medicine-wheel shields. Yarn "grass" is evident on the dancer's outfit in photograph 2.

For innumerable reasons, the origin points of contemporary pow-wow Grass dancing are controversial. After hearing Rendon's story and then reading texts by Clark Wissler (1912, 1916) and William Powers (1963, 1966, 1990), I knew there was a conflict between at least some segments of Lakota oral tradition and written accounts. In conversations with other scholars, additional narratives came to light, including one told to me in 1996 by Edward Wapp (Comanche, Sac/Fox), a professor at the Institute of American Indian Arts. Wapp recalled attending a number of Northern pow-wows in the Dakotas with his family during the late 1950s and seeing the early forms of modern pow-wow Grass dancing there, as performed primarily by Cree people. In his opinion, the form had originated in Canada and gradually migrated south.

That possibility stayed in my mind until August 1997, when I spent a week in the archives of the Buffalo Bill Museum in Cody, Wyoming. There I met Bob Red Elk (Fort Peck Sioux), a museum fellow who told me that, according to his family's knowledge, the Grass Dance had been part of pow-wows for at least a century and until the 1950s was known as "Fancy Grass" to distinguish it from the Omaha Grass version. After a few days of digging through boxes of old photographs yet to be fully archived, I found a photograph album from the 1920s and 1930s filled with a series of small images taken on Pine Ridge Reservation with a Brownie camera. In it there were the unmistakable forms of two Grass dancers, and they wore fringed outfits and eagle-down fluffs attached to their roaches to represent clouds. The caption identified them as "Sioux," and, intriguingly, the regalia they wore appeared to be far closer to that of contemporary dancers than were the examples worn by various models in Powers's books from the early 1960s.

There is no doubt that pow-wow–style Grass dancing was well established on Pine Ridge by the early 1930s and that, based on the automobiles in them, the photographs had been taken no later than the mid-1930s. Considering that Rendon's grandfather would have been a young man at that time and likely first heard his rendition of the story between 1910 and 1920, the dance must have existed on Pine Ridge in a distinctive form even in those years, perhaps as the "young man's" version (chapter 2).

The Jingle Dress Dance

Women's Jingle Dress dancing is a special interest of mine, in large part because I was a Jingle Dress dancer for seven years. Out of respect for the tradition, during that time I learned as much as possible about the meaning of Jingle dancing for both performers and their audiences. One of the most profound elements of Jingle Dress dancing is its spiritual power, which originates as an energy generated from the sound of the cones that sing out to the spirits when dancers lift their feet in time with the drum. The very act of dancing in this dress constitutes a prayer for healing, and often spectators, musicians, and other dancers will make gifts of tobacco to a dancer and request that she pray for an ill family member while she dances. An example of hidden spirituality and ritual within a public forum, the ever-unfolding story of the Jingle Dress Dance is unique in Indian Country. There is little fanfare and no public announcement when the Jingle Dance is performed as a healing prayer, only a quiet circulation of family members from dancer to dancer, a whispered request, and a quick nod of thanks by both parties.

The story of the Jingle Dress Dance begins in Whitefish Bay, a reserve village located on the shores of Lake of the Woods in southwestern Ontario. Small and isolated, it is a Native community where traditional values and sensibilities can still flourish. One of these concepts is that specific kinds of knowledge can be brought into the community through the medium of a dream or vision. Closely tied to this notion is the idea that what the Creator or guardian spirit gives to an individual though a vision is a complete understanding of what they have experienced; there is no need for experimentation or further hypothesis. Older oral narratives, such as that of Crow-Feather (the Pawnee warrior honored by being given the Iruska knowledge in a vision), commonly tell of this experience.

Women in North America have a long history of attaching objects to their clothing in order to make pleasing rhythmic sounds while they danced. In pre-European times, these "jingles" were commonly made from shells, animal teeth, or bone; in the Great Lakes area, women used pieces of hammered copper, a resource abundant in that region. According to photographic evidence from the latter part of the 1800s, Ojibwe women wore decorative sashes trimmed with metal cones, most likely made from scraps of tin cans. Until around 1918 or 1920, however, no specific dance calling for metal cones as part of its regalia existed in Anishnaabeg communities.

Just as the Iruska had its origin in a vision, so, too, did the Jingle Dress Dance. Accounts of its beginnings abound. Unlike many other Native dance forms whose origins are subject to controversy, Jingle dancing can be traced to a specific woman, Maggie White, who was a member of the Whitefish Bay Ojibwe community and died in the early 1990s. The most common Great Lakes–area story of her experience is that the Jingle dress and dance were given to the Anishnaabeg sometime soon after the end of World War I through the medium of White's father's vision, which he sought when she was ill.

It is a fairly simple generic narrative. A young girl was sick and gave no signs of recovering, so her father sought a vision. In that vision he was shown how to make a dress and perform a dance. He set about making the dress and then put it on his daughter and instructed her in the dance. In spite of her illness, she somehow was able to dance, and when she did she was miraculously cured. Afterward, the same girl sought out three other girls and directed each to make a dress in one of the four sacred colors (red, yellow, white, and blue), with four rows of jingles rolled from snuff cans. The girl was Maggie White, and she and the other three girls became the nucleus of the Jingle Dress Dance Society.

The rules of the society were drawn from traditional Ojibwe women's values and concepts of the role of women as caretakers of the family and supporters of men, who in pre-reservation times protected the family from harm. A young woman who wished to join the society was to be of good moral character and a role model of proper behavior. In the year preceding her initiation she was put on a "berry fast" by an older woman and not allowed to eat berries for that year. The fast represented sacrifice and self-discipline. Each day during the fasting year she was to attach one cone to her dress and say a prayer. At the end of the year she was inducted into the Jingle Dress Society and taught the dance. In the Jingle Dance, one foot is never to leave the ground, so the dancer always remains connected to the earth. The society still functions in this same manner, and the dance continues to be performed as prayer of healing.

In the years following its inception, the Jingle Dress Dance became widespread, and alternative narratives can be found in other regions where it is performed. Norma Rendon of Pine Ridge told me of a Lakota example:

> The women's Jingle originated from the Chippewa Tribe. That was right after World War I. This veteran—he was Indian—came back from World War I. Right after that he got sick, he was real sick. He was close to his granddaughter, they had this real tight bond between them. When he got real sick like that, the granddaughter was scared, and she wanted her grandpa to live. So she went to a medicine man, and they went to a ceremony. And she said, "My grandpa is real sick. I hurt inside because he's going to be gone, and I want to know what I can do to make him stay here longer, to be around with me longer." So that medicine man said, "You are his life, his love for you is real strong and the greatest happiness is when he watches you dance." So he said, "What you need to do is to make a dress and on that dress you need to put tins so they'll jingle when you dance. They will sway back and forth and jingle. And when you do that they'll sound like the leaves on your sister the tree. That will calm him [grandfather] and that will heal him. When he sees you dance after that he'll be okay." So she put on a pow-wow and she made her dress. And she went out and she danced. But her dance had to be graceful. Not fast and not slow. And so that's how the Jingle Dress came in, and that's why it's graceful and sways. . . . And after that he [grandfather] saw her dance and was okay. People just started picking it up right after that. (Rendon interview, Aug. 15, 1989)

In this tradition, the power of the dress to heal is still central, but added are the elements of a girl's unique relationship with her grandfather, the medicine man, and the cones sounding like "our sister the tree," recontextualizing the story to better fit a Lakota cultural framework.

Another variant is told by Randy Talmadge (Ho-Chunk), one of the announcers at the Winnebago Standing Rock Summer Ceremonials, a tourist-oriented attraction sponsored by the Ho-Chunk Nation of Wisconsin (the Wisconsin Winnebago have reclaimed the name "Ho-Chunk," their original name for themselves). Talmadge and I worked together on a pow-wow music and dance presentation for the national meeting of the Sonneck Society for American Music in Madison, Wisconsin, in the spring of 1995. Talmadge, who is also a storyteller at Standing Rock, was eager to tell the audience his version of the story.

The Ho-Chunk/Winnebago Jingle Dress tale is similar to the Ojibwe's, but with two important exceptions. First, it is placed within the historic framework of the Anishnaabeg migration from the East, which would date it somewhere close to 1600 C.E. Second, in Talmadge's version the entire Anishnaabeg Confederacy is dying, especially its elders and carriers of tradition, rather than one individual. Talmadge's Jingle Dress legend stresses values and history from a strongly Ho-Chunk viewpoint. It was the Ho-Chunk after all, not the Anishnaabeg, who were nearly wiped out by epidemics during the 1630s. In addition, the Ho-Chunk constantly emphasize the antiquity of their traditions and the more recent arrival to Wisconsin of other tribes. By making it clear that the Anishnaabeg had migrated into the area, the Ho-Chunk can imply that they were there first, an understandable impulse in a state they share with such immigrant tribes as the Oneida, Stockbridge, and Brotherton.

The issue of how to tell variant narratives is not without controversy in the larger Native community. During the summer of 1994, while I was trying to track down a pamphlet containing Maggie White's original narrative, the Whitefish Bay Band council office referred me to Allan Crow, who, I was told, had published the pamphlet. After a brief telephone conversation, I wrote to Crow with details about my research, as he had requested. He replied that he had heard the story of the Jingle Dress and the dance from the woman who wore the dress as a child (Maggie White). When Crow interviewed her, he explained, she had told him that "the story was now [his] and that it could be told in print." Although he included it in the Whitefish Bay pow-wow souvenir booklet, he later told the pow-wow committee to stop selling the booklet because he had not been given proper credit as its author. "I own the rights to the story," Crow asserted. "Any other printed similar to mine is plagiarism." As a professional, published writer, he expected appropriate benefits and credits should he decide to come in with me as a coauthor, he told me on August 9, 1994.

The difficulty presented by Crow's stance is that I do not know what his version is because I have not seen the pamphlet. There is thus no way for me to discern whether I am infringing upon what he considers his cultural property.[1] Because the band council referred me to him, however, I cannot ignore his claims. Based upon his reply, I immediately ceased to seek the pamphlet, a decision made not because I found his answer problematic or was concerned about negotiating with him. Indeed, I accepted his claims of ownership (although I suspect he may have misunderstood my intentions). The larger issue is that once his version of the tale had been published in my book, he unfortunately would no longer be able to control whether it would be plagiarized (in his terminology).

Crow's claims of possession of a now-widespread oral tradition are just one facet of continued Ojibwe attempts to regain authority over the dance and its narratives, in this case by citing the possibility of plagiarism to defend a claim of ownership. Dealing with questions of intellectual property rights for a story told in one variation or another in hundreds of pow-wow programs is akin to controversies of the late 1990s concerning Internet-based music copying programs such as Napster and Gnutella. For better or worse, I suspect that this genie is permanently out of the bottle.

During the half-century following Maggie White's first rendition, the Jingle Dress Dance was limited to the confines of Ojibwe Country and rarely seen other than at pow-wows in those areas. Performed at traditional pow-wows, it subsumed the earlier Women's (Kwe) Dance, taking its shuffle footwork and adding it to the repertoire of the Jingle Dance as a second distinct style. That gives the Jingle Dress Dance two dissimilar footwork styles, "straight" and "round" (also called "side-step," or "shuffle"). Women's Northern Traditional has a similar side-step style, but the tempo and beat pattern of the music for the Jingle Round Dance is unique and unrelated to any other genre of pow-wow song. If an Anishnaabeg Drum can be found, it is rare for one that is not Anishnaabeg to be invited to sing one of these songs. Most Drums, however, can sing the Traditional or straight songs that accompany the more common straight style of dance. For me, the Drum that sings side-step songs with the greatest energy and enthusiasm is the Whitefish Bay Singers, most of whose members are the sons and grandsons of Maggie White.

Not until the late 1960s and early 1970s did the Jingle Dress Dance begin to be seen frequently outside Ojibwe Country. Initially, the only women performing it were Anishnaabeg, but as time went on Northern and Southern Plains women developed an interest in the dance and started to learn it. Because they were not a part of the Anishnaabeg dance tradition, many of these women assembled non-standard dance outfits that had fewer than the required 365 cones and beaded yokes borrowed from Fancy Dance regalia. Moreover, at the grand entry of some western pow-wows, Jingle Dress dancers enter the arena after Fancy dancers, a sign the dance is not accorded the same respect as it is given in Anishnaabeg regions. In addition, footwork in the western states is far different than the careful Anishnaabeg "Woodland" style. Many Plains dancers incorporate spins and lifts reminiscent of the Fancy Dance.

According to pow-wow scuttlebutt, the popularity of Jingle Dress dancing outside traditional Ojibwe communities has caused concern among members of the dance society at Whitefish Bay. On one hand, many consider the dance to be a gift from the Ojibwe to the larger Native North American community. On the other hand, however, the regalia of many women is far beyond that deemed proper, and skin-tight dresses, metallic glitter fabrics, and lace sleeves are coming into vogue (photographs 8 and 9). Many competitive pow-wow dancers also wear eagle feathers, a practice frowned upon by the dance society. For all intents and purposes, the society has lost control of the Jingle Dress Dance and is rumored to be considering a strategy that would return what they consider integrity to it. In a break from tradition, the society may be considering allowing branches to form in other communities and even allowing Indians who are not Anishnaabeg to join.

Fancy Styles

Men's and women's Fancy dancing, although sharing the same name, have somewhat different origins. The men's style developed as a result of intersections between Traditional warrior society dances and Wild West shows, where dancing was performed as an exhibition event for audiences unfamiliar with the meanings behind more (comparatively) sedate styles of war dancing. For the most part, Indians agree that men's Fancy dancing, in the form seen at pow-wows, was first done in Oklahoma after World War I. It gradually spread from there to the Northern Plains and finally to the Great Lakes region during the 1950s. Women's Fancy dancing, sometimes called "Fancy Shawl" or "Butterfly" dancing, either developed shortly before World War II or during the war. Numerous (non-Lakota) oral sources place the dance's birthplace on one of the Lakota reservations in South Dakota. Compared to many other pow-wow dances, the beginnings of men's Fancy and women's Fancy Shawl dancing are not a particularly contested issue. There are slight differences between the Northern and Southern versions of the men's Fancy Dance and essentially none between the North and South in women's Fancy.

Northern Men's Fancy regalia consists of two large bustles, one on the lower back and one on the shoulders. In addition, one *Catabwa* (small bustle) is usually worn on each upper arm. Large bustles generally have dyed feather hackles and ribbons (or tinsel) attached to the end of each feather. Beaded or ribbonwork aprons, yokes, and moccasins or aquasocks, along with spinners in each hand and a roach headdress, make up the rest of the regalia. Two eagle feathers adorn the roach, and it is here that Northern and Southern dancers can be best differentiated. Northern dancers by tradition attach their feathers into what are referred to as "spinners," allowing each feather to move independently. Southern dancers use a device called a "rocker," which is shaped like a horizontal capital *H*. A feather is attached to each end of the top crossbar; the bottom ends of the main bar (which is somewhat shorter than the top bar) attach with rubber bands to make a free-floating "hitch." The result is that the two feathers move together as a single unit, but the rocker moves independently from the dancer's head (photograph 3).

Beyond the requirement of keeping time to the basic drumbeat, Men's Fancy Dance is entirely free-form. Almost anything goes, including splits and cartwheels. Dancers tend to wear colors that are brighter than those used in Traditional styles, and the hackles and fringe attached to their bustle feathers create an effect of constant motion. Fancy dancing has been, and continues to be, a dance of the young. The endurance and athleticism it demands are beyond the abilities of most people by their late thirties. Men's competition Fancy dancing is accompanied by extremely fast music, at times approaching 150 beats per minute and featuring a breathtaking acceleration toward the end of each song. In many ways, images of male Fancy dancers have become iconic of pow-wow dancing (and Indians in general) to the outside world.

Women's Fancy style is a direct outgrowth of male dancing, albeit through an unusual route. According to pow-wow tradition, in the early 1940s a number of teenage girls grew frustrated that only men were permitted to perform the Fancy Dance. In a challenge to convention, they dressed in men's outfits and danced at a South Dakota pow-wow. That and other similar actions led women to develop a Fancy Dance for females. The regalia is simple: a basic dress (or skirt and dress), a yoke, moccasins, leggings, and a shawl worn over the shoulders and arms (photographs 5, 6, and 19).

One common metaphor for the dance is that it represents a caterpillar emerging from her cocoon as a butterfly, just as young girls one day become women. The flowing, spinning motion of the shawl represents the movement of wings. Because it was perfected outside the framework of Traditional styles, women's Fancy Dance breaks with the custom that at least one foot be in touch with the earth. Dancers leap and spin with the spontaneity of youth and the blessing of sound knees. Although somewhat more structured than men's Fancy, and with slower songs, women's Fancy is also a dance of the young. By their mid- to late thirties most women have changed over to performing more sedate dance styles. There are no real differences between Northern and Southern women's Fancy dancers in either regalia or footwork.

I am often asked about gender roles at pow-wows and whether men and women can dance in each other's categories. The answer to that question is a qualified yes, they may. Acceptance of this behavior varies widely, however, depending on the age of the dancer and region where the pow-wow is held. Children are treasured in North American Indian societies and in many ways given more freedom to find themselves during childhood than young people in the dominant culture. Therefore, it is common for girls to be allowed—even encouraged—to dance in boy's outfits through puberty if they wish (chapters 4 and 5). Boys are also seen in female regalia, but far more rarely.

As children grow to adulthood, the question of their dance category begins to tie more and more into concepts of gender identity and sexual orientation. At this point, choice of dance category becomes a statement to the pow-wow community of who a person is and how they wish to be perceived. Indian people tend to be more accepting of difference than the dominant society, primarily because they consider that it is not up to one human to criticize how the Creator has made another. But dancers who are "draggin' it" usually are in for some sideways glances and whispered comments. I have never heard, however, of any dancer not being allowed to dance or being ejected from a pow-wow, harassed, or abused in any way for choosing to dance in a category not traditionally assigned to their sex or gender. Indeed, it is becoming more common for women to Grass Dance, and a few pow-wows are holding special women's Grass Dance competitions. Perhaps in time women's Grass Dance will emerge as its own competition category, with slightly different regalia and footwork than the men's style.

Intertribal Forms

Intertribal dances are those in which members of the audience wearing street clothes may participate. They usually occur in sets early into each pow-wow session and between rounds of contest dancing. Some intertribals are generic pow-wow dances in which participants move slowly clockwise around the arena, often walking and talking. Other intertribals, such as Crow Hops, Round Dances, Two-Steps, Owl Dances, and Snake Dances, are more specialized. In all, participation with friends and family is the key to enjoyment, and the pow-wow's master of ceremonies constantly urges the audience to get out and dance in the arena. At each pow-wow, one man and one women (occasionally, one girl and one boy) are designated as head dancers and given the job of dancing during every intertribal song and being the lead couple for couples' dances. Head dancers keep a pow-wow's action flowing, for without them some intertribal songs would bring no dancers into the arena, particularly in hot, windy, or rainy weather. By custom, no one begins to dance at the beginning of each intertribal "set" until after the head dancers enter into the arena.

The major division among forms of intertribal dancing are between those danced as couples, such as the Two-Step and Owl Dance, and dances where each person technically dances alone, such as Crow Hops, Buffalo Dances (a Southern dance in which dancers are part of a "herd"), Snake Dances, and Round Dances. In Crow Hops and Buffalo Dances each dancer is in independent motion; in Round Dances they are a part in a large, left-moving circle. Snake Dances are somewhat different, for each dancer represents a segment in a giant serpent and follows a leader (normally the male head dancer), who is its "head." At one point the group separates into sections of four people each. Each section dances as a unit as the "snake" crosses a river and then re-forms. Two-Step and Owl Dances are couples' dances, where women choose their partners and men pay if they refuse. For the Two-Step, a lead couple—again the head dancers—choose the steps and set the pace for the rest of the dancers. In the Owl Dance, couples perform independently.

Specials

The most common forms of special exhibition dances at Northern pow-wows are Hoop dancing and Aztec ("Mexica" or "Mexika") dancing. Hoop dancing usually takes place on Sunday afternoons after main competition rounds are over but before prizes are awarded. Aztec dancing is as yet not formally integrated into pow-wows, but often Aztec dance troupes are invited to perform during dinner break for general entertainment purposes and from of a sense of pan-American indigenous solidarity. Neither Hoop nor Aztec dancers are normally paid by the pow-wow committee—other than token amounts of day money—but members of a Hoop dancer's family almost always put out a blanket and collect payment from an appreciative audience.

Historically, the progression of the Hoop Dance from the southwestern Pueblo cultures into the pow-wow circuit is straightforward, in many ways mirroring that of other pow-wow styles. Hoop dancing is a special-

ty and is popular throughout the continental United States. It was originally a religious form of dance in the pueblos of the American Southwest. In the late nineteenth century, however, when tourists began to visit
the pueblos, people there created secular, exhibition versions of previously ceremonial dances. The Hoop Dance was one such display.

Famed throughout the pueblos as the gateway between the Plains and
the Southwest, the pueblo of Taos seems the most likely spot for exhibition Hoop dancing to have entered Plains cultures, and Plains Indians
likely learned the dance there. From the early 1920s onward, Hoop dancing spread in an ever-widening circle across the Plains, picking up a number of Plains characteristics such as the four sacred colors on its way.
Although at one time it was a male-only form, both men and women now
perform the Hoop Dance, with males predominating in numbers. Pre-
teenage girls, however, are taking up the dance with about the same fre-
quency as boys do.

The hoops for the dance, about twenty-four inches in diameter, are
usually decorated in the four sacred colors of the Plains: red, yellow, black,
and white. Those colors, in unity on the hoop, represent what contemporary Native Americans consider the four races of humanity: Indian,
Asian, African, and European. Dancers use the hoops to imitate various
insects and animals, creating an image of human unity. The length of a
Hoop Dance song is controlled by how long it takes the dancers to create a requisite number of abstract forms. Songs are repeated over and over
until a dance is finished. Hoop dancing is extremely difficult to master,
and most performers need at least five years to become competent.

The North American version of contemporary Aztec dancing ("Danza
Azteca" or "Danza Mexika") stems from two sources: the Mexican Indi-
genismo movement in the 1920s and 1930s and surviving elements from
older Mexica cultures, preserved in the styles of Mexican *conchero* dancing. Most of what is known as "Aztec dancing," as seen at North American pow-wows, is an idealized re-creation and reconstruction of dance
forms and music by *folklorico* dance troupes of the 1920s and 1930s who
were looking for symbolic ways to reclaim Mexico's heroic pre-Colum-
bian past. They created a highly theatrical dance form based on surviving Aztec narratives, book illustrations, instruments, and written descrip-
tions of the Spanish conquerors. The Spanish conquered Mexico in 1521,
more than 350 years before American settlers' conquest of the Great
Plains. During those 350 years, traditional Aztec dancing—a religious
tradition—was violently suppressed (and perhaps to a certain extent subsumed) by the Catholic church.

In the United States, family and community-based Aztec dance groups began to form in the early 1970s as an outgrowth of the *la raza* movement. The groups were also motivated by the need for a unique identity, separate from that of the generic "Hispanic," and the urge to connect culturally and spiritually with North American Indians. Unfortunately, many American Aztec dancers are unfamiliar with the history of the genre and have begun to proclaim its antiquity at pow-wows and in interviews with Indian-oriented newspapers. According to Carlos Casteneda of Denver's Grupo Tlaloc, for example, contemporary North American Aztec dancing springs from the direct survival of ancient Aztec forms: "This is a handed-down oral tradition from our grandmothers and grandfathers. . . . The dances are done by memory. It is a teaching of balance, harmony, respect for everything around us and our environment. Whenever we come together in a circle, we try to teach what has not been taught in schools. . . . Dating back to the Maya and Aztec empires, the religious dances have survived Spanish colonialism and modern times" (Arias 1999:22).

Despite such claims, North American Aztec dancing is not the result of uninterrupted oral transmission and continuity across generations, direct from earlier Aztec culture. It is is folklorico-based and has few if any connections with Nahuatl-speaking communities in Mexico. Although it is unclear whether any of the musical traditions still exist in an unadulterated form (some instruments do survive in museums), some of the customary dance steps and music may survive in rural Mexico, as suggested by Ines Hernadez-Avila in her ongoing research on the Mexican conchero dance tradition (also known as "Aztec dance" in Mexico).

Chris Goertzen (2001:85) has described the "tightly choreographed display dances by visiting troupes of Aztec dancers" at pow-wows in the piedmont of North Carolina. Troupes are composed of "extended families from Mexico who make a living at U.S. Latin-American Festivals and pow-wows." Although the dancers identified themselves to Goertzen as "pure Aztecs," the mother of one told him that they were actually Tarascans. Thus it seems that groups of Mexican dancers are traveling the small pow-wow circuit as the ubiquitous Peruvian pan-pipe bands have since the 1980s. It is possible that these dancers, unlike their North American counterparts, have ties to the Mexican conchero tradition—and indeed may in some sense be true Aztec dancers. In creating a niche for themselves in areas that do not have large Chicana and Chicano populations or locally based Aztec dancers, Mexican performers may eventually bring about a cultural cross-fertilization with American troupes.

Southern Dance Styles at Northern Pow-wows

It is common to see Southern dancers (such as myself) at Northern pow-wows. Eastern Oklahoma's Prairie tribes have generated two dances specific to that region: men's Southern Straight and women's Southern Cloth Dance. Both have origins in the Dream Dance movement of the late 1890s and have aesthetically similar regalia, fitting together historically as a pair in the same manner as men's and Women's (Buckskin) Northern Traditional styles. Southern Straight and Cloth Traditional dancers are less flamboyant in dress and footwork than their Northern counterparts, favoring a "clean" look with far fewer feathers and fringes. While Northern dancers wear fully beaded outfits, Southerners use ribbonwork and rows of beads set off with paint and metal spots. Spatial organization and the textures of exposed areas between beaded bands are very important to the Southern aesthetic, a concept that holds true on a larger scale throughout their regalia fashions.

Southern Straight dancers wear long shirts, leggings, wide belts, and thick leather drops covered with conchos, aprons of trade cloth, bandoliers, and a roach or turban (photograph 4). Each man carries a fan in his left hand and a beaded pointing stick in his right that he uses to follow a "trail." Footwork is subdued and conservative. Women's Southern Cloth dancers wear a long shirt (with no belt), a trade-cloth (generally selvage-edge) skirt, ribbonwork drop, leggings, and moccasins. They also drape a shawl over their left arms and a purse over their right wrists and hold a fan in their right hands. Options include a scarf, rows of silver brooches, and a half-size (compared to Northern Traditional) bone breastplate. Their footwork is a stylized walk, with straight-backed upper-body posture and elbows bent somewhat outward so the shawl's fringe has room to swing.

New Dance Categories at Northern Pow-wows

Since the late 1980s, a number of new categories and one new competition dance have entered the pow-wow circuit. Because of rapid changes in the regalia and footwork of some men's Traditional and Grass dancers (essentially a "fancying-up") at many large events, these styles have been split into two sub-styles: Contemporary and Old. Northeastern dances have split further because male Iroquoian dancers at times compete in the Eastern Straight category. To call this style of dancing "Straight" is a misnomer. The term *Straight* in a pow-wow context refers as much to the act of following a trail, dance stick in hand, as it does to the lack of a back bustle (evidently the inspiration for the category's name). Although it is understandable that men want to compete in a separate category from Plains-oriented men's Traditional—because their regalia and footwork are so different from judging norms—another name for their dance would be more appropriate. By calling the dance style "Straight" they do disservice to Southern men who perform the Oklahoma-originated dance.

Indian people of the Northeast (Iroquois, Penobscot, Miq-Maq, and Pequot) have, since the early 1990s, expressed great desire to have one of their styles incorporated into pow-wow competition. At a number of larger Northeastern Dances, Smoke dancing has moved from a special to a regular contest for both men and women. According to Kyle Dowdy, Sr. (Seneca), a professional Smoke Dance singer, the dance was given to the Iroquois by the Oklahoma Osage tribe and is a version of the Osage Fast War Dance. That story seems improbable, but Senecas (one of the Six Iroquois nations) do live in northeastern Oklahoma, close to the Osage reservation. Intermarriage and other cultural contacts might well have facilitated the gift of the dance style from the Osage to the Oklahoma Seneca. After that, it would have been only a matter of time for it to spread from the Oklahoma Seneca to the Northeastern Seneca and then throughout the Iroquoian Confederacy. Smoke dancing uses a single singer who plays a waterdrum in a series of fast songs requiring fancy footwork. As further verification of Dowdy's tale, although the music at first sounds quite different from standard pow-wow songs, its interior form and structure are almost exactly the same (chapter 4).

4 *Making and Singing Songs*

On the North American pow-wow circuit, Drum groups iden-
tify themselves as singing in one of two broad regional performance styles:
Northern or Southern. The Northern-style area includes Drums from the
Central and Northern Great Plains, Canada, and the Great Lakes regions;
Southern singing is found in Oklahoma and parts of Wisconsin (Ho-
Chunk) and Nebraska (Omaha).[1] Outside of those areas, choice of singing style can vary greatly and depend on a number of factors, including
personal style preferences and the presence of influential singers not
native to the region in which they live. Beyond those circumstances, a
powerful determinant is the affinity in performance-practice of a singer's tribal-specific singing tradition with either the Northern or Southern vocal style. I have noticed over the years that many Iroquoian Drums
sing Southern songs, whereas Navajo groups often sing Northern. That
phenomenon cannot be fully explained by geographic proximity, migra-
tion/relocation patterns, or intermarriage. It may just be that people tend
to sing songs they are vocally comfortable with performing. In both cases
(Navajo and Iroquoian), the pow-wow singing style most often chosen is
the one that more closely resembles a tribal-specific repertory.

Participants at Northern pow-wows have their own characteristic
ways of singing and dancing, and within this larger framework exist regional and tribal customs that in the past made dances in each locale
distinct from those in other areas. At the present, however, music performed by Indian singers at pow-wows, although it still spreads through
oral culture, is transmitted via cassette tapes and compact discs. In many
cases, Northern pow-wow singers learn as much from commercial re-

leases and self-made recordings of other Drums that play at pow-wows as they do from the members of their own tribes, which increases the tendency toward a generic, "Northern" sound.

Most pow-wow singers cannot read music. Even if they do, they refuse to learn new repertoire in that way. To use Western terminology, Native pow-wow musicians "learn by ear," and for that reason very little of what I write about in this chapter will have meaning for most of them other than perhaps as a matter of intellectual curiosity. Due to those factors, my intention is to provide a "map" of the music for those who do not perform it, beginning with an overview and critique of scholarly research and continuing with discussions of pow-wow drums as instruments, performance aesthetics, and musical form and analysis from both Western and Indian viewpoints.

As an ethnomusicologist, one of my primary goals in studying pow-wow music has been to take songs and divide them into smaller parts according to the rules of Western formal analysis. At the same time, in the experiences and aesthetics of most Native singers and dancers, these songs are perceived as being complete entities. As Simon Ortiz articulates this conflict, "A song really does not break down into separate elements. In the minds and views of the people singing it at my home or in a Navajo religious ceremony, for whatever purpose a song is meant and used, whether it be for prayer, a dancing event, or as part of a story, the song does not break down. It is part of the complete voice of a person" (1977:3). With those words in mind, I can write with confidence that Indians (with the exception of a few Native ethnomusicologists) do not hear pow-wow songs in the pieces and parts into which I will parse them. In fact, many may reject this kind of analysis completely and consider it to be a kind of intellectual or musical colonization. Yet those who repudiate musical transcriptions as a form of discussion should know that I mean no disrespect. Rather, as my teaching experience has shown me, some non-Indian people cannot follow the music unless it is broken down for them.

It is my hope that many issues raised by members of the Indian community concerning academic and scholarly respect for their musical culture can be resolved by a meeting of Western terminology with Native performance traditions and sensibilities. Indian ways of talking about music and dance are metaphoric as well as descriptive, and layers of meaning are often lost when Western musical terminology is indiscriminately applied.

Another major problem in discussing indigenous music—indeed, *any* music—is that of intellectual property rights. U.S. laws generally do not respect the copyright of any music defined as "folk," and, for now, pow-wow music is considered folk music unless it has been copyrighted when recorded. Although many singers may not realize it, their recording companies, after making a cassette or compact disc, may hold the copyright to their songs. Indians, however, do have a very strong sense of song ownership, especially when the song belongs to an individual or family. Further confusing the issue, when I transcribe a song, legally the written transcription is my "interpretation" of that song and does not violate copyright.

Navigating these uncertain waters, the songs that I decided to transcribe for this chapter exist, to the best of my knowledge, in the realm of "open" songs—that is, none belong to an individual or a family. I have heard each one in multiple contexts: at a minimum of two pow-wows and as performed by different Drums. By contrast, the two songs in chapters 6 and 7 do belong to individuals or Drums and have been transcribed with permission.

Historical Perspectives in Scholarly Research

The established formal structure of pow-wow music, originating from the Omaha Nation's Heluska War Dance, has remained relatively unchanged since the 1950s. This form, most often termed "incomplete repetition" by scholars (Nettl 1954:25; Vennum 1989:8) and "Traditional" or "War Dance" by Native singers, has distinctive Northern and Southern variations. Specific dance movements (including footwork) are associated with each style. Most early accounts (before 1880) of War Dance musical styles focused upon how the music sounded to non-Indian ears rather than how it was formally organized. As a result, analytical discourse about the development of early, reservation-era Grass Dance forms into contemporary pow-wow styles must rely primarily on a study of early field recordings and transcriptions, extrapolation from modern styles claiming continuous usage from earlier times, and Native oral tradition.

Orin Hatton has outlined four general periods of Grass/Omaha Dance performance: development and diffusion (1840–90), common practice (1890–1920), Northern (1920–45), and regional (1945–70). He also suggests that the early 1970s mark the beginning of a fifth period (1986:202–3).[2] Recordings and reliable transcriptions are rare and late in the period for the first period (almost exclusively from Alice Fletcher and Francis LaFleshe) and limited for the second and third. By comparing field recordings Frances Densmore made of the Teton Sioux between 1911 and 1914 and of the Skidi and Chaui Pawnee in 1919 and 1920 with those Willard

Rhodes made thirty years later (the Sioux between 1940 and 1947, the Kiowa in 1941, and the Kiowa and Pawnee in 1951), a series of musical adjustments and changes evident through the second and third periods culminate in modern formal structures.[3]

In 1916 Densmore, who in photograph 10 plays an early wax cylinder recording for Mountain Chief (Blackfoot), recorded songs of the types ancestral to both Northern and Southern pow-wow styles during the second period. Her recordings of Pawnee War Dance songs (1951a) and Sioux Grass Dance songs (1951b), show that short, repetitive phrases with Native-language texts broken by formulaic, cadential patterns sung in vocables are characteristic of both. Except for the replacement of some texts by vocables, those characteristics also hold for contemporary pow-wow songs. In one photograph of a typical Northern Drum from this period (1911), men sit on the ground around the drum and female singers form a semicircle behind them (photograph 11). One of the greatest problems with early field recordings is apparent when comparing photographs 10 and 11: Wax cylinder recording equipment was limited to capturing a few singers at a time and only for shorter songs. War Dance performance practice, however, involved large-group singing and was unconducive to being recorded by cylinder machines.

By the time Rhodes was in the field, Northern and Southern styles had greatly diverged. Southern War Dance songs maintained honor beats (a series of drum accents) in the same place as earlier Omaha Heluska songs but added an optional "rise": a half-step modulation after the first full repeat (Rhodes 1954a, 1954b). In Northern songs, at that time still called "Omaha songs," the honor beats were moved to an internal position, coinciding with the second cadential pattern (Rhodes 1954c; see also Issacs [1959:108]; and music examples 2 and 3 in this volume). Those traits are key to distinguishing between modern Northern Traditional/ Straight song and Southern War Dance styles.[4]

By the mid-1950s, anthropologists and ethnomusicologists had begun referring to the musical form used in pow-wow dance songs—both Northern and Southern—as "incomplete repetition form," a practice that still continues. Thomas Vennum, Jr., for example, has analyzed Ojibwe (Northern) pow-wow songs:

> One constant feature of songs on Side A [of a cassette tape] is their structure. A song is typically begun by the lead singer who is interrupted partway through his phrase by the other members, who complete the phrase. Then a number of musical phrases follow, each pitched slightly lower than the previous one, until a musical cadence is reached in the lower part of the singers' range. At this point, the singers go back to the begin-

ning of the melody but omit the first (A) phrase. This produces what students of American Indian music have come to call "incomplete repetition" form, which can be represented as AA1BCD/BCD. . . . It is now customary to close with a final coda or "tail" which is simply a final incomplete repetition, preceded by a brief break in the drumming to signal the end of the song. (1989:8)

William Powers, a scholar of Oglala (Lakota) music and culture, also initially analyzed Northern Plains War Dance song form as an incomplete repetition, although he spells it as AA1BCBC/BCBC (1990:117).[5] In some of his more recent writings, however, Powers suggests for study a "synthetic model" that considers Oglala musical conceptualizations for inclusion as part of the ethnomusicological vocabulary. "The Oglala do not distinguish between theme and cadence," he notes (1980:39, 30). The reasons for the different spellings of the same form by Vennum and Powers become apparent in figure 3. Vennum is describing the form of an Ojibwe/Ottawa (Great Lakes and Minnesota) variant of the Grass Dance form and using letters to delineate complete phrases. Powers, however, sketches the more widespread Northern Plains template but separates cadential patterns from larger phrases as the letter *C*.

An intriguing examination (which he terms a "cultural analysis") of Gros Ventre war expedition songs by Orin Hatton offers "a model structured by the paradigm of creation and the paradigmatic relations that comprise the speech continuum—thought:breath:speech:crying:singing" (1988:80). Hatton's examples of war expedition songs use the same form as Grass Dance songs, although some of the Gros Ventre songs are more compact (1988:96, 100). Hatton's analysis adds a metaphysical dimension to the songs, "Converge[ing] specific instrumental relations within the paradigm of creation" (95) and suggesting the values of "announcement" for the A phrases, "thought" for the B phrases, and "closure" for the C phrase.

Hatton's "cultural analysis" deals with the musical genre of Gros Ventre war expedition songs, which use the same form as Northern Plains Grass/Omaha songs. Although war expedition songs undoubtedly existed in Gros Ventre society before they took up the Grass Dance between 1875 and 1880 (Hatton 1986:200), Hatton offers no evidence that pre–Grass Dance war expedition songs used the Grass Dance form. Yet his "model for cultural analysis of Gros Ventre music" (1988:80) is not only Gros Ventre–specific but also form-specific: "The model is structured by the paradigm of creation and the paradigmatic relations that comprise the speech continuum. . . . Singing invests creative works with formality and respect, and represents an intensification of speech and crying. . . . The

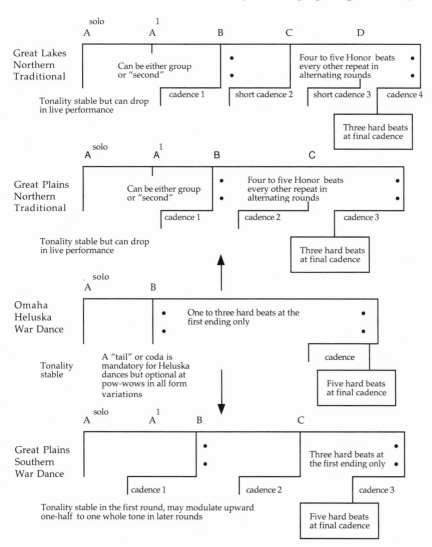

Figure 3. Omaha Musical Form

paradigm of creation provides the structure of both singing and song. The model for analysis of singing is thus crying intensified, and song is structured by the paradigm of creation as well" (1988:80).

Hatton's model invites further study, for it suggests that the Gros Ventre may have invested spiritual meaning in a primarily secular song form that did not originate within their culture. That concept is being contested on the pow-wow circuit, where the possibility of sacred meaning in a public event is advocated by some and rejected by others.

Making the Instruments

At smaller Northern pow-wows, the drums most often seen are old, commercial, marching-band bass drums; at larger events, more recognized Drums tend to have handcrafted instruments. Ludwig seems to be the commercial brand of choice, probably because Ludwig Drums of Chicago is an established firm and many used Ludwig drums are available. Commercial drums usually are equipped with heavy cowhide heads for indoor and outdoor summer use. The original plastic (mylar) heads are retained on some instruments meant for outdoor use, however, because plastic heads function well in humid, wet weather. Drums are generally twenty-six or twenty-eight inches by eighteen inches; tuned low and with have some slack in the head to create a deeper-pitched sound; and muffled with duct tape. Drums that have skin heads are generally tuned to a higher pitch, because natural animal rawhide is far less durable than plastic under heavy use and when the head is slack or damp it easily rips or can be punched through. Occasionally, a drum might be covered with elk hide rather than cowhide. Elk hide is more expensive and difficult to obtain than cowhide, but to a certain extent a drum is more powerful—both in sound and spirit—if covered with elk. Other, more rare, types of drum are fully handcrafted and have custom-made stands. Old-style octagonal dance drums are flat and shallow and have eight sides suspended by four straps attached to four poles. The sound produced by this drum is high and almost without resonance; when struck, an octagonal drum makes a sound closer to buzzing than a tone. Because the sound they make lacks carrying power, octagonal drums are rarely seen at large outdoor pow-wows unless they have been miked.

Most drums and many drumheads are painted or taped with traditional designs that have meaning to the players and honor the drum; marching band–style bass drums are often wrapped in embroidered cloth or buckskin to disguise their previous function. Drums treated in a traditional way are kept in special enclosures ("drum houses") when not in use. When taken out for performance, the drum will be treated with the consideration due a living entity and given gifts of tobacco. In photograph 12, the Porcupine Singers (Pine Ridge Reservation) sit and sing at their drum. Between each pow-wow session the drum is carefully and respectfully covered (photograph 13).

Drumsticks come in a variety of shapes and sizes, with the Northern versions generally longer than the Southern. The shafts of sticks range from fourteen to twenty inches long and from one-half to three-fourths of an inch in diameter; the wrapped playing ends are from one and one-half to two inches in diameter. Shafts are made of tree branches, birch dowels, or fiberglass fishing rods. Because of their flexibility and ability to rebound, fishing rods are the modern material of choice; the ends that strike the drum are wrapped in wool, leather, or white faux fur. Like drums, drumsticks are usually decorated in some way, most often by being wrapped with colored tape.

Vocal Styles and Musical Aesthetics

A Drum is made up of anywhere from three to twelve (or more) men and women who sing together on a regular basis. "Sitting at the drum" is primarily a male activity, and women, most of the time, stand behind the men and sing the "women's part" an octave higher than the men and with little or no vocal vibrato. In some all-female Drum groups women sing the "men's part," but those groups are rare and, as of this writing, exclusively Northern.

Although gender-based restrictions on female singing at first seem arbitrary and perhaps sexist, they are rooted in pragmatic performance needs and governed in both Northern and Southern performance styles by aesthetic preference and acoustics. High sounds are directional. If women sit at the drum rather than stand behind the men, their contribution to the music—which is considerable—is buried in the drum's booming tones and by the bodies of the men who sit across from them. When women do sit at the drum, they sing the same part as the men, something entirely possible in Northern singing but almost impossible in Southern performance. Almost no woman would be capable of singing the full range of Southern style.

At pow-wow gatherings a Drum's regular singers can be joined by friends, acquaintances, or members of other Drums. The desired vocal quality of a Northern singer is high and tight with a heavy vibrato or even more widely spaced pulsation. When they sing high, Northern singers use their chest voices rather than their throat voices in a male falsetto. Good singers place the beginnings of vocables or words between drumbeats as often as possible. That technique, which makes a voice more audible, is called "singing off the beat" and is one of the elements that creates rhythmic complexity in pow-wow music. In addition, a good singer keeps a steady beat, knows the entire song repertoire, and plays the drum at a volume level balanced with that of the vocal volume level. Good Drums meet these criteria and also sing and play with precision. These attributes all combine to create the Indian musical ideal of "harmony," a balance among singers, drum, and song that allows the Drum to function smoothly as a single unit.

Talking about Music

Like other American music, pow-wow music uses a primarily Western musical vocabulary. Because pow-wow music exists in a pan-tribal (as opposed to tribal-specific) context, musicians use English when talking about song-making and performance and also employ some terms in common with those of Western music. Yet even when a word exists in both musical worlds its meaning can differ markedly. "Harmony" is glossed in Western formal analysis as a vertical sonority, but among Native Americans it describes how singers adjust the strength of their accompanying drum stroke so no one person will play louder than the others at a Drum. Terminology can also be deceptive. "One beat," for example, is a common tempo designation among dancers on the Northern Plains. The phrase is not, however, a fixed value. It indicates an ideal tempo for that particular region's dancers. Every reservation's "one-beat" is *its* concept of a good tempo for dancing. The music of neighboring tribes (to the north or south) is generally "half a beat" faster or slower, even though those same neighbors, when asked, will say, "Our music has a speed of one-beat." The meaning of "melody," however, is the same to all Indian musicians and equivalent to that of performers in Western contexts.

Although a number of publications detailing Northern Grass Dance form variants have been produced since the 1970s, Southern styles, including the prototype Omaha Heluska songs, have received much less attention. Although my personal interests originally were oriented more toward Northern songs, I have come to believe that one style cannot be discussed without introducing others and therefore use three diverse examples of War Dance songs for comparative purposes: Omaha Heluska, Southern, and Northern. Two primary features help dancers differentiate between Northern and Southern pow-wow songs. First, overall ranges are different. Northern songs begin and end at higher pitches than Southern ones (ex. 1). Second, the overall formal structure of each type is distinctive enough to be considered a variation of the inceptive form, the Heluska (He'thu'shka) song. The basis for both Northern Grass/ Omaha Dance songs and Southern O'ho-ma society songs is found in the Omaha Nation's Heluska War Dance songs (fig. 3).[6] In modern pow-wow

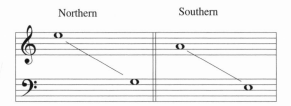

Music example 1. Comparative Vocal Ranges in
Northern and Southern Styles

terminology, these song types are named respectively Traditional (which
includes Native-language-text, also known as "word," songs) or Straight
(made up entirely of vocables) in the north and War Dance songs in the
south. Because both the older and the contemporary variations of these
song forms derive from the Omaha Heluska Dance, I have chosen to refer to the overarching form as "Omaha form," with the Northern variation subtitled "Traditional/Straight" and the Southern, "War Dance."
Pow-wow performers use this same terminology and recognize the important role played by the Omaha people in disseminating the old warrior society and its songs during the 1800s.

Most pow-wow songs are strophic and have an interior repetition. In
Indians' performance terminology, dancers call each strophe a "round";
singers use the term *push-up*.[7] "Push-up" refers to pushing the voice to
a higher pitch at the beginning of each new strophe and is descriptive of
the physical effort of singing, something a term such as *incomplete repetition* does not relate to those unfamiliar with Native performance practices. Indian singers and dancers perceive each push-up or round as a
complete musical whole, whereas an "incomplete repetition" divides the
strophe into two discrete parts. Where Indians hear four push-ups (the
traditional number required for a dance performance), Western analysis
recognizes eight repetitions, four complete and four incomplete.

The phrases indicated by letters in figure 3 are delineated by either a
repeat or a cadential pattern. The form spelling of one complete round
of a contemporary War Dance or Straight Dance song is AA1/BC/BC for
the Great Plains variant and AA1BCD/BCD for the Great Lakes variant.
These spellings agree with Vennum and Powers's statement that "the
Oglala do not distinguish between theme and cadence" (1980:30). They
do not, however, agree with Powers's spelling—AA1BCBC/BCBC—which
includes cadential patterns. The older (but still in use) Omaha Heluska
form used in the songs of the Omaha Nation's Heluska (Brave Man or Man
Dance) warrior society is a simpler A/B/B (fig. 3).

The well-known Heluska "Wakonda" song (ex. 2) was a pow-wow grand entry song and has been transcribed from a taped performance of the Milwaukee Bucks Drum (Ho-Chunk/Winnebago) at the Milwaukee Midwinter Pow-wow in 1994. A typical Heluska song, it begins with an initial series of drumbeats that allow singers to synchronize with dancers and then opens with a solo declaration of the theme (A) by the head singer. This solo melodic entrance is common to all pow-wow songs and functions as an incipit, signaling and assuring other singers about what song is to be performed. The other members of the Drum first echo the opening phrase (A) exactly and then begin a series of variations, moving down the scale and completing the B section with a formulaic, cadential pattern made up of straight-sixteenth notes and three "hard beats" (a musician's term) or "honor beats" (a dancer's term) that separate the interior repeats. When performed at an actual Heluska Dance event, the numbers of hard beats between interior repeats can vary from one to three. More important, the tail, which is optional in pow-wow performances, is mandatory at a Heluska Dance. The silent space between it and the end of the final round must be long enough for all dancers except the "tail dancer" to take their seats. Only the tail dancer is allowed to dance during the tail, along with those who have paid for the privilege of dancing with him.

The Southern War Dance song (ex. 3) is typical of songs that have been sung in Oklahoma since the end of World War II. When the Omaha Heluska warrior society was taken up by the Comanche and Kiowa, they referred to its music and dances as "O'ho-ma" (a mispronunciation of Omaha). Although the Kiowa and Comanche spread the warrior society from tribe to tribe in the post-reservation era, the geographic distance between tribal groups in Oklahoma is much less than in the North, allowing fewer deviations from the original Heluska style. In addition, the Oklahoma Ponca and the Omaha share the same language and music. Until the 1860s the Ponca were part of the greater Omaha Nation and have been influential in maintaining Heluska songs in the South. Because of those factors (and others), Hatton's historic periods in Grass Dance performance are not applicable to Southern musical practices.

The overall song structure of music example 3 is similar to the Northern Straight style with the exception of honor/hard-beat placement that occurs between repeats in the manner of a Heluska song. At the conclusion of the first round, however, the overall pitch modulates half a step upward, exactly as in the Pawnee war song that Rhodes recorded in 1951 (Rhodes 1954b). Southern War Dance cadences are in even-sixteenth notes, and their rhythmic and vocable design vary little from that of the

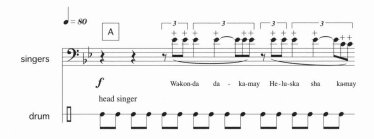

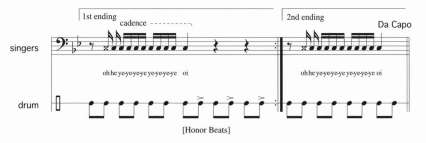

Music example 2. Heluska "Wakonda" Song, Transcribed from a Performance by the Milwaukee Bucks Singers (Ho-Chunk)

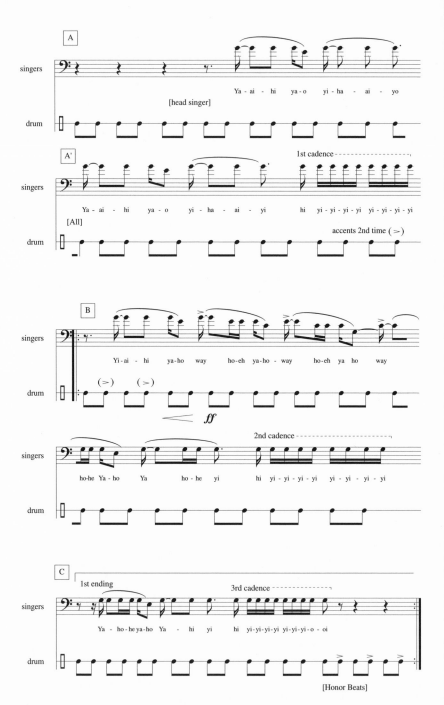

Music example 3. Southern War Song, Transcribed from a Performance of the Alliance West Singers (Kiowa/Comanche)

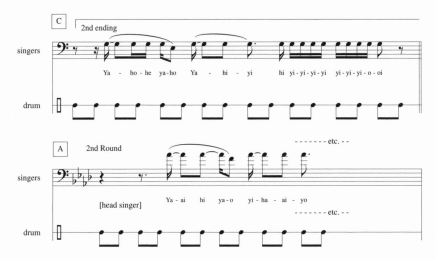

Music example 3. Con't.

Heluska song's single cadence. Only the third cadence in each Northern song uses even-sixteenths, whereas the first two in all tribal-specific variations contain some kind of syncopation and an assortment of vocables. In the Southern style, hard beats are played at a slightly faster tempo than the rest of the music from the second round onward (if the song was originally made as a war song). If the song belongs to a family or individual, then its hard beats are played at the same tempo as the body of the song throughout the performance.

Although the Milwaukee Bucks are a Winnebago/Ho-Chunk Drum and sing in a predominantly Southern style, Wisconsin Ho-Chunk (the Wisconsin branch of the tribe has reclaimed their traditional name) also are capable of singing in the Northern style favored by their Ojibwe and Menomini neighbors. A Northern Straight song was sung for the Girl's Fancy Shawl Dance competition at the 1989 Ann Arbor Pow-wow by the Bear Clan Singers, a Winnebago/Ho-Chunk Drum made up of members of the Cleveland family of Waukesha, Wisconsin (ex. 4). Because they sing throughout the Great Lakes region, the Bear Clan Singers have a large repertoire of songs suitable for any pow-wow.

Although music example 4 is technically a Northern song in form and honor-beat placement, its limited range and non-standard cadential patterns suggest that it is a hybrid. Intended for a competition among girls aged seven to twelve, the song's length and melodic simplicity are unusual, although its exact adherence to formal norms is typical of a song

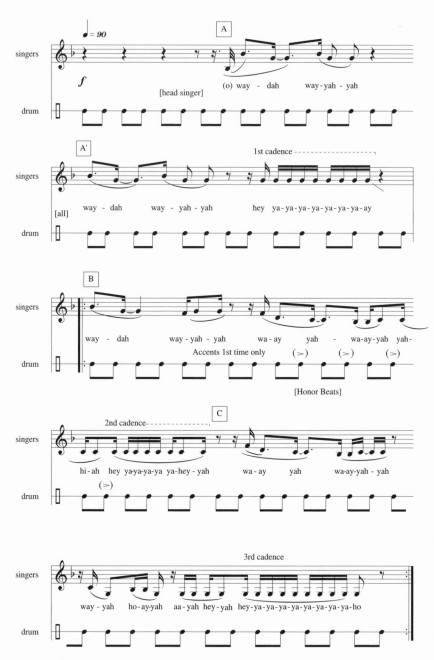

Music example 4. Northern Straight Song for Girl's Fancy Dance, Transcribed from a Performance by the Bear Clan Singers (Ho-Chunk)

meant for competition dancing. As in the Heluska song, this Straight song begins with an opening solo statement of the theme (A), which is followed with a "second" by the entire group (A1). In contrast to the Heluska song, however, the second is completed by a cadential pattern that marks the first large phrase grouping and the starting point of the interior repetition (B/C). Four to five honor beats are within the song itself rather than between repeats. They traditionally occur only the first time through so as not to obscure the Native-language texts sometimes heard during the second repeat.

During the live performances of many Northern songs, overall tonality modulates downward, approximately a quarter tone at each new entrance (A, A1, B), and usually stabilizes around B. That is because head Northern singers attempt to push the upper range of songs to the highest pitch possible, something other singers are often unable to sustain after an opening melodic statement. The Bear Clan Singers, however, are at heart a Southern Drum, and the Southern songs that make up their repertoire are pitch-stable in the first round. Southern Drums traditionally sing in a lower vocal range and do not participate in the "higher is better" aesthetic common to the Northern pow-wow circuit. Their performances of Northern songs reflects that practice.

After listening and dancing to enough Northern songs, it became clear that far more than language use distinguished the music of one nation from another. Beyond differences in range and formal structure, Northern and Southern songs use slightly divergent cadence patterns. The Northern cadence patterns in music example 5, organized by tribal group, are not meant as absolutes but only as examples of commonly used patterns. I have included for comparative purposes two Southern cadential patterns in music example 6.

As a rule, Northern music has more rhythm and melody (in the form of microtones) than Southern. The Northern variant of the Omaha form spread over a greater geographic area, which allowed for modification to fit local mores. The length and number of large phrases (two to three used after the introductory section of a song) in Northern music also tend to be static. Perhaps phrase numbers and lengths vary more in Southern music because of the musician-dancer relationship. When dancing and listening to Southern songs, it is easy to hear a formal separation of their sections because of the location and solo nature of hard beats. In Northern songs, however, those hard or honor beats are often difficult to distinguish from other accented notes. Thus it is far easier for dancers to follow Southern songs and be able to anticipate their endings—even when a song has five internal phrases.

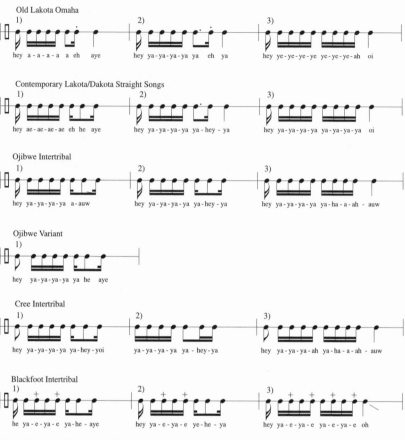

Old Lakota Omaha

1) hey a - a - a - a ah eh aye
2) hey ya - ya - ya - ya ya eh ya
3) hey ye - ye - ye - ye ye - ye - ye - ah oi

Contemporary Lakota/Dakota Straight Songs

1) hey ae - ae - ae - ae eh he aye
2) hey ya - ya - ya - ya ya - hey - ya
3) hey ya - ya - ya - ya ya - ya - ya - ya oi

Ojibwe Intertribal

1) hey ya - ya - ya - ya a - auw
2) hey ya - ya - ya - ya ya - hey - ya
3) hey ya - ya - ya - ya ya - ha - a - ah - auw

Ojibwe Variant

1) hey ya - ya - ya - ya ya he aye

Cree Intertribal

1) hey ya - ya - ya - ya ya - hey - yoi
2) ya - ya - ya - ya ya - hey - ya
3) hey ya - ya - ya - ah ya - ha - a - ah - auw

Blackfoot Intertribal

1) he ya - e - ya - e ya - he - aye
2) hey ya - e - ya - e ye - he - ya
3) hey ya - e - ya - e ya - e - ya - e oh

Music example 5. Northern Cadential Patterns

Ponca Heluska Song

3) he ye - ye - ye - ye ye - ye - ye - ye oi

Kiowa/Comanche War Dance Songs

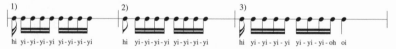

1) hi yi - yi - yi - yi yi - yi - yi - yi
2) hi yi - yi - yi - yi yi - yi - yi - yi
3) hi yi - yi - yi - yi yi - yi - yi - oh oi

Music example 6. Southern Cadential Patterns

In addition to the War Dance/Omaha–form songs discussed so far, two other song categories are common at Northern pow-wows: Crow Hops and social dance songs. In addition to form and text, a primary determinant of song type is the organization of its underlying rhythmic pulsation pattern into either duple or triple meter and the relationship of that pattern to a dancer's footwork. Based upon dancer footwork, I have coined the expressions *single beat, double beat,* and *triple beat* to characterize the linkage between dancers and songs. In Western terms, these would be described as two variations on duple-meter (single and double) and triple-meter pulsation. War Dance/Omaha–form songs are always double beat, and close to 95 percent of Northern songs (traditional, word, intertribal, and straight) use the Omaha form.

Most single-beat songs at Northern events are from the genre known as Crow Hops (ex. 7) The transcription in music example 7 is of an old, widely known Lakota song. According to many contemporary pow-wow narratives, Crow Hop songs (and dance footwork) originated with the Crow Nation of Montana. There are, however, problems with that scenario. First, the Crows' name for themselves is "Absaroke." The term *Crow* was not attached to them until the mid-1800s—and by white traders and settlers at that. Second, a very similar Southern song style is called the Horse Stealing/Horse Trot Dance, and it has nothing to do with the

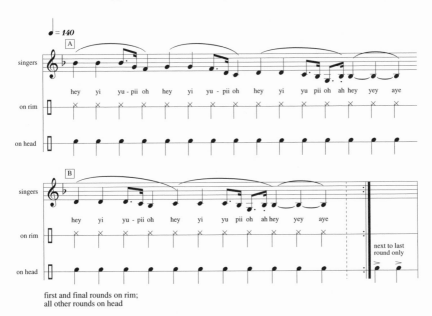

Music example 7. Traditional Crow Hop (Lakota)

Crow Nation. But then again, perhaps that dance was indeed in some way associated with the Absaroke, and the Kiowa (who at one time were part of the Absaroke) took the dance with them when they migrated south hundreds of years ago and called it the Horse Trot. Because the dance is widespread, its place of origin may never be known. At Northern pow-wows, Crow Hops can be used to accompany women's Fancy, women's Jingle, and male Traditional dancers in competition and, more generally, in intertribal rounds.

At Northern pow-wows, triple-beat songs are almost entirely associated with social dancing, with the exception of the women's Traditional Side-step. With that pulsation pattern, dancers take steps either on beats one and three (men and women) or on beat one (Traditional women). An excerpt of a classic Round Dance, "Indian Girls," is given in music example 8, with sample intertribal footwork written under the drum notation. One other song classification is that of "mixed beat," in which musicians include a variety of beat patterns, usually drum rolls with random hard-beat accents followed by sections of duple-meter-beat War Dance music. These songs are danced almost exclusively by male Traditional and Fancy dancers, although some women perform them during intertribals (fig. 4).

Music example 8. "Indian Girls" Round Dance

	Northern	Southern
Single beat	Flag songs Crow Hops Snake Dance songs	Flag songs Horse Trot songs Horse Stealing songs
Double beat	Traditional songs Straight songs "Pow-wow" songs Intertribal songs War Dance songs Jingle Dance songs a. Shuffle b. Round c. Two-step	Fast War Dance songs Slow War Dance songs (for straight dancers)
Triple beat	Round Dance songs Two-step songs Owl Dance songs "49" songs	War Mother songs Soldier Dance songs Round Dance songs 49/War Journey songs Two-step songs Scalp dance
Mixed beats	Sneak-up songs	Buffalo Dance songs

Figure 4. Music and Dance Terminology

Songs, Dancing, and Footwork

Without dancers performing to it, pow-wow music as a distinctive form would almost surely cease to exist. This music, although enjoyable to listen to on its own, lives and evolves in tandem with dancers, reacting to their preferences and needs. Drums constantly communicate with dancers through a series of musical signals, beginning with the basic pulsation pattern and including hard or honor beats, other drum accents, crescendos and decrescendos (becoming gradually louder or softer), and tempo changes (speed). The relationship between music and dancer in its most fundamental form, and kinesthetically realized as footwork, provides a graphic illustration of drumbeat pulsation patterns (fig. 5). Figure 5 is meant to convey the footwork used during intertribals, not contest rounds, and includes the common variations between men's and women's footwork.

After three rounds, songs generally end, their final rounds beginning at a much softer dynamic level and a gradual crescendo until a series of accents. Singers who play songs that lack tails almost always to use a crescendo to remind dancers that the music will soon cease. The ideal, however, is not always the reality. According to Norma Rendon:

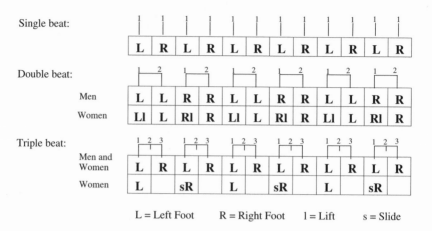

Figure 5. Footwork and Music

They'll [the Drum] have a succession, like four sets. . . . The head singer, he sings and then the background comes in, and they sing out the rest of the song, and that's one set. So then they'll say "Four sets, four rounds," and that's the sing. But sometimes they don't have ears, and they'll go on to a fifth or sixth set, so you have to be careful. You can try and watch the Drum, but sometimes you can't. Watch that lead singer's finger on his stick start coming back up again, and you'll know he isn't going to stop—but you can't always watch him. (Interview, August 15, 1989)

Songs that have tails pause briefly between the end of the final set and the tail in order to signal that the end is close. Often that pause saves contest dancers who have lost track of the number of rounds from dancing though the song's final beats.

Within each Northern song is a series of honor beats, usually four or five hard beats that are played every other round. As Norma Rendon told me on August 15, 1989, "When they do those honor beats, then the dancers will raise their fans. And what they are doing is they're honoring their people, they're honoring the veterans, anybody who has ever been in war, and *Tunkashila,* the Great Spirit. And those four honor beats are for the People. Among our tribe [Lakota] only the oldest woman from each family has the right to raise her fan on those honor beats. Also, if your father or one of your brothers or uncle or grandpa was a veteran, then you have the right to raise your fan."

Rendon is specific about four being the correct number of honor beats in the Northern style. Most often, however, a preparatory hard beat signals dancers that the four honor beats are immanent. Honor-beat sequences are set up in a variety of song types, and Northern single- and double-beat patterns use a preparatory hard beat (fig. 6). Some singers and dancers consider that beat to be part of the honor-beat sequence, although others, such as Rendon, do not.

Music and Meaning

Bruno Nettl (1989:170) has, after Merriam, posed a question: "Is there a Blackfoot Theory Text?" His question is also pertinent to contemporary pow-wow music. Clearly, pow-wow music has established concepts of history, function, and musicianship—all categories within Nettl's definition. In addition, the songs have strict yet flexible formal and rhythmic guidelines and operate within a clearly defined performance setting. Moreover, performers (dancers and singers) organize their repertoires into defined categories. All of those elements are hallmarks of an internalized oral theory text.

What do the songs mean to those who perform them? The most basic answer is that the texts of many songs often refer to historical events. Then again, what about songs without words? Are they just ordinary dance music, like that found in other social settings around the world? When approaching a pow-wow, long before the singing is heard or the dancers are seen, there is the drumbeat itself. It echoes out into the sky and rumbles down through the earth, representing the heartbeat of all humanity. Over and over when I ask singers and dancers about their pow-wow experiences they refer to the drum and the power of its sound. Unlike Western music, where instruments usually accompany vocalists and music is a backdrop for dancing, song and dance at pow-wows accompany the drum.

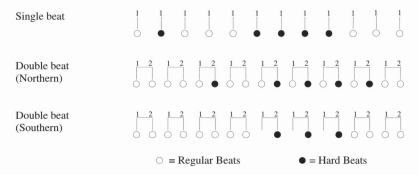

Figure 6. Honor-beat Patterns

5   *Pow-wows in Space and Time*

Pow-wows inhabit a varied and complex number of domains, depending on the perceptions of individual participants. Because affairs run according to a pre-set schedule, they unfold in accordance to a fixed clock time (despite the "Indian time" comments of announcers) primarily determined by the order of events. That assures participants that pow-wows will share certain similarities and allows for the fundamental bottom-up (as opposed to top-down) organization of Dances. Exclusive of the need for events to run on schedule, a true Indian time does exist at pow-wows, and it grows out of the cyclic nature of song forms and the dance circle itself. The spatial layout of the dance arena and its surroundings are also significant. They can be viewed as physical arrangements of people and objects, as cultural metaphors, and as a nexus between spiritual and physical worlds inhabited by beings unseen and unknowable.

Pow-wows by Schedule and Tradition

Although contests and traditional events share many of the same characteristics, the demands of competition can alter the basic sequence of events at a pow-wow, sometimes in profound ways. Traditional pow-wows, not bound by the requirements of holding a certain number of contest rounds (usually four per dance category), have far more flexibility in scheduling specials and more exotic types of intertribal dances such as Snake or Buffalo Dances, where participants can dance who are not wearing regalia. But a contest pow-wow is obligated to have one or two opening contest rounds for all who enter in a specific category and one or two final rounds the next day if requested by the judges. Often, if the point system is designed poorly, dancers who have tied in points for a specific place (either first, second, or third) must participate in a final "dance-off," which further takes the time that could be used for inter-tribals or specials.[1]

The competition segment of a pow-wow is run by an individual designated as the "head judge" (or head judges, sometimes as many as three). The head judge or judges create the point system used and delegate much of the judging to seasoned dancers capable of appraising dancers outside their competition category. These "on-the-spot" judges are called to the podium just before a contest round. Usually, each is given a score card listing the number of places (first, second, third, and honorable mention) and then awards a certain number of points for each. Presumably, judging is based upon set criteria such as footwork (and staying with the music) and regalia. Judges have the right to ask for a second competition song and designate what type it will be. They often do and request songs that showcase a different style of footwork than in the initial song. Many medium-to-large-size pow-wows also have Drum contests at which members of the head Drum serve as judges.

Judges bring to their job their personal aesthetic standards and relationships with those whom they will assess. Because of the latter, a good head judge will attempt (as much as possible) to keep individuals from judging friends and relatives. Each competing dancer has an assigned number, and judges note rankings (first, second, and third) in boxes on scorecards. Each box represents a number of points. Between the first and second days of an event points are totaled, and a specific number of dancers, usually eight, becomes eligible for the final rounds. Points are also "taken" (i.e., given) at grand entry and at some intertribals and figure into deciding who will dance in the final rounds as well as the ultimate order of placement.

A representative order of events for a single-day pow-wow, or for the complete Saturday of a two-day Dance less the awarding of prizes, is given in table 1. Most two-day (Saturday and Sunday) pow-wows begin at 1 P.M. on Saturday with the grand entry, a processional in which all dancers must participate if they intend to compete because points are taken as the dancers enter the arena.[2] One of the head Drums sings grand entry songs for as many rounds as needed for all dancers to come into the arena.[3] If a grand entry is extremely long, head Drums will trade off singing. Typically, dancers enter in the following order: the head veteran, who carries the eagle feather staff; other flag carriers (all veteran male and female); the head dancers for that pow-wow (or session); any pow-wow

Table 1. Pow-wow Order of Events

1. Grand Entry
   a. Dancers enter in the following orders:

Variation 1	Variation 2
Flag Bearers/Color Guard	Flag Bearers/Color Guard
Optional: Honored Guests and Elders	Optional: Honored Guests and Elders
Head Dancers	Head Dancers
Pow-wow Princess	Pow-wow Princess
Men Traditional Dancers	Men Traditional Dancers
Women Traditional Dancers	Men Grass Dancers
(1) Buckskin Dancers	Men Fancy Dancers
(2) Cloth Dancers	Boy Traditional Dancers
Men Grass Dancers	Boy Grass Dancers
Women Jingle Dancers	Boy Fancy Dancers
Men Fancy Dancers	Women Traditional Dancers
Women Fancy Dancers	(1) Buckskin Dancers
Boy Traditional Dancers	(2) Cloth Dancers
Girl Traditional Dancers	Women Jingle Dancers
(1) Buckskin Dancers	Women Fancy Dancers
(2) Cloth Dancers	Girl Traditional Dancers
Boy Grass Dancers	(1) Buckskin Dancers
Girl Jingle Dancers	(2) Cloth Dancers
Boy Fancy Dancers	Girl Jingle Dancers
Girl Fancy Dancers	Girl Fancy Dancers

   b. Flag Songs
   c. Invocation/Prayer
   d. Posting of Colors
2. a. Veterans' Dance
   b. Intertribals
3. Exhibition Dances (by age)
   a. Tiny Tots: Both genders (exhibition doubles as competition)
   b. 7–12: Traditional, Grass, Jingle, Fancy
   c. 13–17: Traditional, Grass, Jingle, Fancy
   d. 18–44: Traditional, Grass, Jingle, Fancy
   e. 44+ ("Golden Age"): Traditional, Grass, Jingle, Fancy
4. Intertribals
5. Retire Colors

Dinner Break

6. Second Grand Entry (same as 1)
7. a. Veterans' Dance
   b. Intertribals
8. Competition Dances (same order as exhibition dances)
9. Specials
10. Intertribals
11. Awards
12. Retire Colors

princesses in attendance; adult male dancers; adult female dancers; boys; and then girls. An alternate order involves all male dancers, including boys, then all female dancers, including girls. Dancers in each category enter eldest to youngest, and those wearing Buckskin regalia enter before those dressed for the Cloth categories. As dancers of each category move past the announcer's location, he (I have never encountered a female announcer) enthusiastically introduces them to the audience.

The choice of grand entry order depends on the arena director, and in some cases their personal preferences and tribal affiliations can have an effect. For example, although in women's categories the dancers who wear buckskin outfits traditionally enter before those who wear cloth, at one pow-wow in Los Angeles the arena director—a respected television actor—called Southern Cloth dancers to enter before the other women.

After the grand entry, all present stand for the flag song, which most Indians consider to be the equivalent of a tribal National Anthem. Most nations have their own song, and Drums sing the flag song of their tribe rather than the flag song most closely associated with tribes living in the region of the pow-wow. Following next is the invocation, usually a welcoming of the guests and a prayer, sometimes in the speaker's indigenous language, other times in English. Opening events conclude with a posting of individual flags as the names of veterans carrying each flag are called out and each is asked to "post their colors." By custom, the eagle feather staff is posted first, then national flags (United States, Canada, and Mexico), and finally the flags of various branches of the Armed Forces.

At nearly all Northern events, the first song performed after the opening collection of dances and speeches is the veteran's song, and all veterans, regardless of race or heritage, are asked to dance in the arena and be honored for their willingness to give their lives to protect others. Then open dancing resumes with a long session of intertribals, usually at least ten to twelve songs. During this time a Drum rotation is established, and Drums take turns singing in predetermined order. This custom makes sure that each Drum has an equal opportunity to sing and also gives them an idea of when they will perform so they can leave the drums for food, shopping, socializing, and, at indoor events, smoking outdoors.

Most intertribal dances are accompanied by slow Straight songs and move clockwise around the arena in the style of a War Dance. Social dances—those accompanied by triple-beat songs—work somewhat differently. There are three major types of triple-beat social dancing, the Round Dance, Two-Step, and 49 (fig. 7). The 49—an Indian-only social gathering—occurs after pow-wows and is technically not part of the event. Because the 49 is mentioned so often in conjunction with pow-wows, however, a brief reference is in order. Round Dances, known to some as "Friendship Dances," move in a large, clockwise circle that occasionally has two parts, an interior, men's circle and an exterior, women's circle. Dancers face inward and slide to their left. For a Two-Step (or Owl Dance), participants form couples, men on the left, and move forward, either following a lead couple (in the Two-Step) or independently (in the Owl Dance). A 49 features a series of concentric rings. Participants link elbows and move inward (the location of the hand drummer or singers) as they move to the left. Two-Step and Round Dance songs are for the most part interchangeable and can also be featured at 49s. Special Oklahoma 49 songs ("war journey songs"), however, are specific and are not to be used to accompany Round Dances or Two-Steps.

After the sets of intertribal songs, each category of dancers is called out for an exhibition. Exhibition dance rounds often compress multiple categories—such as men's Grass and Traditional or women's Jingle and Fancy—into a single event to save time. The song tempos for each are similar. A few intertribal songs are often after the exhibitions, and then the contest rounds begin. A second Drum rotation is often established for contest songs. Competition moves from youngest to oldest dancers and begins with the "tiny tots," children from birth to four (babies may be carried by their mothers). All tiny tot competitors win, and all receive a prize, usually $5 to $10 and some candy. Initial contest rounds are used to choose finalists for the second day of dances, although all tiny tots perform the second day. More intertribal dancing follows the preliminary contest rounds for boys' and girls' contests, and the Drum rotation picks up where it had left off with last series of intertribal dances.

The second Saturday session almost always begins at 7 P.M. with a

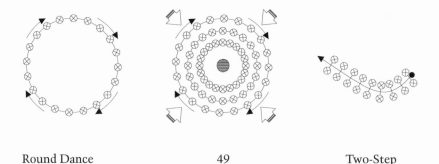

Round Dance   49   Two-Step

Figure 7. Triple-beat Social Dances

eties is that prestige comes through acts of giving and not the accumulation of wealth.

Memorials are special dance competitions to honor someone who has died and usually are scheduled about a year after that person's passing. These competitions are separate from the pow-wow contests and have Drums and judges that have been selected by the family of the deceased. Before the competition begins, a relative or close friend of the person being remembered gives a short account of that person's life and accomplishments. Memorial Dance competitions are only for designated categories of dancers, and prize money is awarded immediately at the conclusion of the competition. After that, there is an Honor Dance of some kind. Not only do Memorial Dances honor the deceased, but they also they mark the end of a mourning period in a dignified and celebratory way.

The most common unscheduled special is a dance required when a participant drops an eagle feather. When that happens, the feather can only be picked up by a veteran (usually the head veteran), who, along with three other veterans, then dances in honor of the fallen warrior represented by the feather. When the dance concludes, the head veteran picks up the feather and returns it to the dancer who dropped it. Songs sung during this ritual are called "Charging the Feather" songs. The dance is an embarrassment to the dancer who dropped the feather, who often will not claim it. They must, however, in one way or the other give it away. One explanation among many for this tradition is that when an eagle drops a feather and a human picks it up, the eagle does not return to demand the feather back. Therefore, neither should a human who drops an eagle feather expect it to be returned. Many dancers also talk about dropped eagle feathers in terms of caring for regalia and assume that those who are careless in attaching them are prone to dropping feathers. I have never seen an eagle feather dropped by a woman, although, to be fair, women wear far fewer feathers than men.

Dance Arena Spatial Organizations

The grounds for each pow-wow, including the arena and its surrounding areas, are laid out according to a preconceived blueprint and create a consecrated performance space for participants. Pow-wow grounds are blessed by members—usually the elders—of each community, who perform that function by burning tobacco or sage, an act accompanied by prayers and songs. By doing so the grounds are cleared of negative spirits and influences, a business of utmost importance because consecrated spaces are considered neutral grounds where all personal hostilities are to be put aside. Before the grand entry begins, many dancers personally cleanse themselves and their regalia by smoking braids of sweet grass and often circulate around the arena, burning braids in hand, and offer smoke to any who wish it.

The two ways of organizing pow-wow grounds at Northern events are based upon the cultural metaphors of the Sacred Hoop and the Sacred Fire. For a Lakota pow-wow, grounds are organized by the physical and spatial metaphor of the Sacred Hoop (fig. 8). The Sacred Hoop is a series of layers arranged from the inside to the outside in a way that physically demonstrates the core values of Lakota society. In pre-reservation days, the primary duty of warriors was to protect children, women, and elders. To assist in that, Lakota encampments were organized in a series of circles and the more vulnerable members of the tribe set up camp at the interior.

The spatial organization of contemporary Lakota pow-wows mirrors encampments of previous centuries. Women dance clockwise and occupy the center of the circle, and male dancers move around them in the opposite direction, representing a protective force. The next layer is the Drums, which symbolize a protective hoop around the entire arena. Ex-

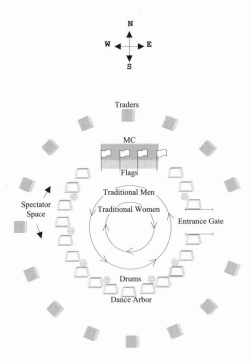

Figure 8. Lakota Pow-wow Space

tending outward are further layers: the dance arbor (a shaded resting area), spectators, and traders (photograph 7). Commonly found on the Northern and Central Plains, this ordering is also customary in the intermountain and Pacific Northwest regions.

Anishnaabeg pow-wow grounds are also traditionally arranged in a series of enveloping circles (fig. 9). Drum groups set up at the middle of the arena (or under an arbor if outdoors) and symbolize the central sacred fire of the Anishnaabeg Confederation (photograph 14). This arrangement is also common to Southern (Oklahoma) pow-wows. If possible, flags (colors) are posted in a half-circle around the Drums. At Anishnaabeg events, men and women both dance in the same direction, clockwise, although more active dancers tend toward the arena's outer edges and men often dance in a circle surrounding women. The next layer is made up of dancer's families and friends, then come spectators, and then traders. Between the families and the non-Indian spectators lurk "pow-wow potatoes," Indians of all ages who attend pow-wows for food, entertainment, and "snagging" (meeting those of the opposite sex).[4]

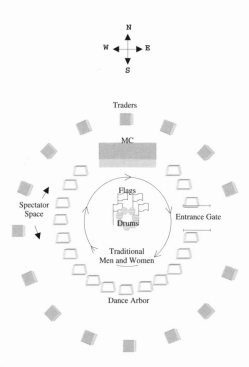

Figure 9. Anishnaabeg Pow-wow Space

Spatial Metaphors for a Spiritual Realm

In September 1997, the last time I completed a taped interview of the Martin and Shananaquet families at their homes on the Rabbit River, George Martin said relatively little. As I talked with his son-in-law David and his daughter Punkin, he sat quietly, drawing. After nearly five minutes he handed me a small paper with a penned diagram (fig. 10). I have juxtaposed Martin's diagram with "Typical non-Indian Perception of Pow-wow Space," which is based upon the ten years of student pow-wow report papers I have read. Perhaps the most profound difference between the two is Martin's recognition and location of a final protective layer of spirits. Through that belief he bridges the invisible membrane between physical (seen) and spiritual (unseen) realms. Many Indians speak about ancestors being present at pow-wows and dancing along with them, joining worlds with a drumbeat sounding simultaneously in both.

Severt Young Bear delineates four circles at reservation based Lakota pow-wows (*wacipi*): dancers at the center of the arena and Drums; involved audience members seated in lawn chairs; young people interacting; and the uninvolved "outer ring that has those who are in the dark" (Young Bear and Theisz 1994:177). Young Bear is speaking metaphorically about Lakota identity and cultural understanding. Larger, more urban pow-wows, however, are often the only Native-sanctified spaces that participants encounter. Dancing in a great circle, they unite as one people to the beat of the drum. Songs are cyclic and represent the continuity of time and life itself. The symbolic number four is given life by the

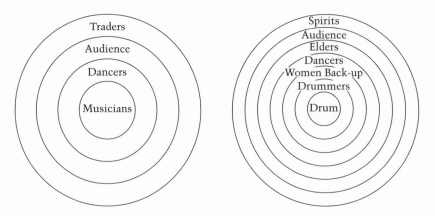

Figure 10. Typical non-Indian Perception and Meaning of Pow-wow Space (left) and George Martin's (Ojibwe) Concept of Pow-wow Space (right)

music's organization: four rounds to a song, four honor beats played within the round. Thus the four sacred directions, the four sacred colors of red, yellow, black, and white, and the four worlds of the Creation—the earth, the land, the air, and the sky—are represented, acknowledged, and honored by the songs and those who dance to them.

6 The Dancing of Six Generations: Lakol Wicoh'an Ki Wastélaka Imacage (I have grown up liking the Lakota ways)

I have known Norma Rendon and her family since 1986, when we first met while students at the University of Colorado, Boulder. At the time she had four children: Chanda, Aspen, and Robert Rendon and January Little. She has since added two more, Nadine and Ardie Janis, in addition to Zeno, her *takoja* (grandson). All are members of the Oglala Lakota Nation, whose home reservation is Pine Ridge in southwestern South Dakota. Norma works as the children's advocate for Cangleska, a women's shelter in Kyle, one of the larger towns on Pine Ridge. She has taught at Porcupine Day School and is certified as a bilingual teacher in Lakota and English. Norma, Jan, Nadine, Ardie, and Zeno live on the reservation in the town of Porcupine (where Chanda lives during the summers); Chanda and Aspen are students at Fort Lewis College in Colorado; and Robert lives in Denver, where he is a Web page designer for US West (photograph 21).

Norma, her children, and her grandson come from a long line of professional dancers and musicians, beginning with her great-grandfather Amos Little (Iron Hawk, photograph 15). At times, she, too, has made part of her living on the pow-wow circuit. The family would arrive at a pow-wow with very little money, knowing that at least one of them would have to win or place so the rest could make their way home. "Somehow," she said, "one of us always did." Those days are now in the past, and the Rendons pow-wow for enjoyment (although prize money is still a good thing, *enit*).

The two interviews that follow were conducted in August 1997 during the afternoon of the fourth day of my planned four-day stay at Norma's home in Porcupine. We needed to get to Rosebud Fair that evening and had spent the first three days doing the important work of shopping, visiting friends, hanging out by the reservoir, visiting more friends, and staying home with coffee and toast in case anyone came to visit us— which they did. The traditions of "visiting" and hospitality remain essentially unchanged in Lakota life (and on other reservations as well) from the last century, when people lived in camp circles and dropped in unannounced on those staying in the lodge next door. Visiting in 1999 was no different except that "next door" in the late twentieth century might be thirty miles away. Visits are brief, often less than thirty minutes in length, and seemingly on whim. By mid-afternoon on any given day, half of Pine Ridge seems to be on the road, headed out on their visiting rounds, while the other half waits at home for the visitors, coffee and snacks (fried chicken for the lucky) ready and waiting on the table.

For someone like me, an outsider to reservation life, the idea of moving to Pine Ridge—which Norma did in the early 1990s—was incomprehensible, and I was baffled by her tales of contentment, especially because she had previously lived in cities such as Denver and Boulder. Why willingly settle in a region repeatedly cited as being the "poorest county in America"? For me, visiting was a key to understanding the place—as well as anyone from urban California could "understand" Pine Ridge. It was small-town life writ large—doors unlocked, friends entering and exiting at will, and everyone knowing everyone else. Unfortunately, the stream of guests was so constant that we finally had to conduct the interviews in her bedroom with the door locked.

Luckily for me, Robert was able to drive up from Denver, and we spoke first while Norma conducted some last-minute visits with friends in the town of Pine Ridge. My conversations with each are quite different in tone, possibly because Norma regularly speaks in public as part of her job, whereas Robert does not. I had a specific list of questions for Robert based upon my curiosity about aspects of musical performance and was motivated by a desire to create a comparative framework for my interview with David Shananaquet, an Ottawa singer (chapter 6). In general, Norma controlled the flow of her narrative, whereas I was more active in Robert's discussion of music.

Norma Rendon

FAMILY HISTORY

Norma: I started dancing when I was a very young girl. In our family, as soon as you can walk, you start dancing. That was always our form of entertainment during family get-togethers. We also used to go to pow-wows when I was a little girl.

The first pair of moccasins I got was beaded for me by my grandfather, Wallace Little [photograph 16]. He was from Oglala, South Dakota, and that's where I spent my summers—when I was a little girl, that's where I was raised. Grandpa [Wallace] and my grandma, Millie, raised me. She was a Traditional dancer, and he was a Traditional dancer. My Uncle Bob was a Fancy dancer, and he also used to be a Hoop dancer. A long time ago there were quite a few Hoop dancers, but he was one of the most well-known dancers. He traveled, they all traveled, to Europe and always performed at Cheyenne Frontier Days. My great-grandfather, Amos Little, who was also known as Iron Hawk, he traveled with a Wild West show and went over to Europe and danced all over the place. So dancing has always been a part of our family's tradition.

Back then, though, the pow-wows are a lot different than they are today. I remember the families would all camp together. We all camped by each other. And I remember we would do what was called the "Little Dance." So our family would come in the arena. My grandfather would lead us in, then my grandma, then the boys, then the girls, then the grandchildren.

Tara: Is this actually the "Little Dance" for the Little family?

Norma: Yes, for the Little family. If it was a Red Cloud Dance, then it would be the Red Cloud family, or it would be the White Eyes family, so it would be the White Eyes Dance.

But the family would come out, and the song would actually be to honor that family. It was the community's way of being able to pay the Drums. So, say we chose Sons of the Oglalas as our Drum to sing the song for our family because my grandfather wanted to honor his grandchildren, he wanted to honor his children, he wanted to honor his wife. So he did a dance in honor of his family, where as he goes around the circle, people would come and give him money. When the song's over, that money goes to that Drum. So maybe if the White Eyes family would pick Sons of the Oglala, then we'll call on Porcupine Singers to sing our honor song. Then people would come and give them money, and then that money would go to that Drum, because back then there weren't contests. But people still needed the financial assistance to get to the pow-wows. So the Drums were kind of paid that way.

Tara: Can you give me a span of years that you're talking about?

Norma: Well, that was before I was in school. So that . . . [laughter].

Tara: She doesn't want to give me a year [laughter]. Come on, give me approximate years.

Norma: Approximately, about the early sixties, '59 through '60, '61, around there. At that time they had rations, so every morning in front of your tent you'd have meat and potatoes and even commodities, but you'd have a bag of groceries that was right there. And the communities [holding the dances] fed. You had food when you got there. You didn't have to worry about eating. And they had—I don't even remember what they call it, but at night I always remember feeling safe because we'd go—after the pow-wow's over—go back to your camp, get ready for bed and be laying in bed. And there would be singers that would come to your door, they were called "doorway singers." They'd come to every camp, and they would sing songs all night long as they would go around. So we had different types of singers, too. They weren't 49 songs, they weren't 49 singers. They would just sing honor songs, and songs like that all night, warrior songs, Warrior Dance songs, stuff like that, all night long and go to the different camps.

There were a lot of camps at that time. And they used white canvas tents with sticks, I remember that. There was a lot of tradition that came with it back then. They talk about, how each *tiyospaye* has different rules when it comes to singing and dancing. And [tiyospaye] that just means family. Tiyospaye is your family. They have different rules—each tiyospaye has different rules, so whatever I say, this is what my grandfather taught me, and this is what we went by in our family.

One of the things my grandfather always told me as I grew older, he said, "Ladies and men, when they're starting to bead, have matching leggings, moccasins, their top matches, all their beadwork matches." And he said, "Don't ever do this, my girl, because nothing's ever the same in this world and no two people are ever the same. And your life doesn't just go on an even keel. There's going to be ups and downs and nothing is ever the same, so your beadwork should reflect that." We're very colorful people, and that means you put different colors in your outfit. You don't just have everything matching. Red with the blue and the yellow and the white in it, your main color red. "Don't do things like that," he said.

"Always stay colorful." And his regalia always showed that. Back then, he used to wear different-colored long-johns in his outfit, either yellow or he had red. He did his own beadwork, he did his own outfit. At that time, everybody did their own. And he's the one who tried to show me how to bead, but actually my mother in the end taught me.

My mother and my aunt, Dawn Little Sky, showed me a lot about beading. So I've done my own beadwork, and my children do their own beadwork. I've got the younger ones to teach yet how to bead. We take pride in the fact that you make up your own design, and you do your own work. And it's good. I'm glad he [Grandfather] taught me all of that. He taught me how to make moccasins, and he said the reason for that is I would never be without shoes—so he taught me. But back then they still did a lot of their own tanning of hides—they still had a lot of our ways back then. Now it's too expensive to buy your own leather, and it's a little bit more expensive now than it was back then. They did their own. They went hunting, they did their own hides and everything back then still, or my family did anyway. And I just used to love to dance. It was a big, happy time for me. So as I grew older and the society changed I still can look back and remember those happy times.

MUSIC AND SPIRITUAL POWER

Norma: When I'm feeling depressed, or if I'm having a hard time, the main thing that will get me out of that is a pow-wow. I don't care what is going on in my life, if I'm at a pow-wow I'm happy. And that happiness is from the music. The people are there, the music is there, our words are there, our ways are strong, and they're powerful. Those ways are what gives us strength to continue on and to live a good life, and I think that's what pow-wows are all about. They're changed today from what they were back then. But still the people are there, the songs are there, the words of the different nations—the different Indian nations—are there. And the strength, the veterans' songs, the honoring of the woman, the honoring of the man, the honoring of the children, all those songs are there. In those songs it talks about communities and being strong and staying together. It gives you strength when you hear these songs.

A good example for that comes from my son Robert, who was a firefighter. A few weeks back I was introduced to this guy that was a firefighter with him [Robert]. He was talking about this huge fire in Oregon that they were fighting one summer, and he said they were out longer than the hours they were supposed to be out. Everybody was tired. He said it felt like nobody could go on anymore, and then Robert picked up this bag and threw it over his shoulder. He started singing Lakota, he started singing songs, and words of the People. It gave them all strength to get up this hill they had to get up. And they had to get up that hill because the fire was coming. But because of those words in that song, and because of the song itself, it gave all the men the strength to get up that hill. So we have very powerful ways among our people. And they were given to us for a reason.

That's the same with the drum. My grandfather said he never wanted to see me sitting at that drum. The women in our family cannot sit at a drum. Everybody's different, again I want to stress that. Do you see women sitting at a drum? Well, maybe they have the right to sit at that drum, but in my family we don't. And he [Grandfather] said the reason is because of the four circles. The first circle is the drum. The second circle are the men that sit behind that drum. The third circle are the women that stand behind the men and sing. And the fourth circle is the People. If you take them out of that context you lose the power. And for me, it's true. I could sit at a drum with five men and my singing would blend right in with theirs. You wouldn't be able to hear me over those men. I could stand behind a drum of sixteen men, and if I'm standing behind them you'll hear me over those men. The things that my grandfather taught me have always been true, have always come true, and I believe in everything that he's ever taught me. Everything. I believe that every one of our ways is for a reason.

POW-WOWS

Norma: I first was a Fancy dancer, and now that I'm older I'm a Traditional dancer. But when my children were growing up, my girls and I used to Fancy dance together. That's how they learned—they learned from me. Now my younger children are learning from the older children. So it's just something that gets passed down from generation to generation.

As I grew older, I learned about 49 songs. And I really loved 49 songs. Those originated in Oklahoma, and they really know how to 49 in Oklahoma. We have some real beautiful 49 songs ourselves, and we 49 up here. I heard that [the 49] started a long time ago. I think it was during World War I or World War II, one of those wars. There were fifty—this was told to me by Arlen Rhodes, who's from Oklahoma—he said there were fifty-some soldiers from Oklahoma, Indian men, that went to battle together. And they said, "After the war is over we'll meet back here. We'll celebrate, we'll sing, and we'll dance, and we'll bring the People together. We'll have a big pow-wow and together, we'll be together again." So they came back. But when they got back and the war was over, there were only forty-nine of them. So there was a song sung for each one of those warriors—forty-nine songs sung. From that day on they just called it a 49, and that was out of Oklahoma so it has spread. These were songs that were sung after the pow-wow.

There is a lot of tradition that comes with pow-wows. Like the men Traditional dancers, they wear the feathers. The women wear feathers in their hair—the ones that carry fans. Those feathers are treated with respect. My son was taught that you should always smudge—and my girls—you should always smudge your feathers and plumes before you dance. Take the time to pray for that eagle that those feathers came from. When you're done dancing, you should smudge them again and put them [feathers] away in a proper place where they will be taken care of. And there shouldn't be any alcohol or drugs around these feathers. A woman that's on her time shouldn't be around them—not because that's a bad thing but because she's real powerful during that time. So out of respect for those feathers they should be smudged. My son [Robert] was told, as long as you smudge these feathers you'll never drop them. Take good care of them, you pray for them, you smudge them, you'll never drop that feather. The whole life he's had of dancing he's always smudged his feathers. There was one time that he didn't smudge his feathers, and there's only been one time that he's ever dropped them. When he came back, it hurt. It hurt me to see his feathers fall and hit the ground, and it hurt him that I could see it. I can't even explain the feeling that you feel when that happens, because I cried. I was so hurt that those feathers hit the ground that I cried. He gave away his *pesa* [roach] and his two feathers up on the top.

When we went home that evening his head was hanging, and I knew that he was depressed. I told him there wasn't anything he could do about it. He tied it on, it came loose, it happened, it's over with, we had a giveaway for it. He gave away a part of his outfit. Everything was good after that. And he told me, "This was the one time that I didn't smudge my feathers. I was in such a rush to get to grand entry." So, our ways, the different things my grandfather taught me, are real strong.

COMPARATIVE MUSIC AND DANCE TRADITIONS

Norma: And then there are different styles. Even with Indian people in the North, just like the ones here—how we sing and dance is different than it is further north. Further north they're almost a half a beat slower. And this same music here is just a beat faster, half a beat faster. I can hear the difference. After you dance a long time, and you sing a long time, you can feel the difference there.

Tara: By further north, do you mean Cheyenne River? Or further north than that?

Norma: Further north. I'd say around Bismarck, Ft. Thompson, especially toward Canada.

Tara: Is music faster in Oklahoma then?

Norma: Oh, yeah. Well, for the Fancy dancers the music is faster. But not for the Traditionals. The Traditionals, they might be only about a half a beat faster.

Tara: All right. What we have to do here is figure out how fast the beat is. So what I want to do is, I'll hold the mike and then have you do something like this. Is this beat here [taps 130 beats per minute], and this is this beat farther north [taps 138 beats per minute]? Okay?

Norma: That's about right just what you did.

Tara: About this fast? [Taps 130 beats per minute.]

Norma: Yeah.

Tara: Is that about here? [Taps.]

Norma: Yeah.

Tara: So farther north it's about [taps 138 beats per minute]?

Norma: Yeah

Tara: Okay, because the concept of a beat and its speed is interesting.

Norma: It would depend on the song. We've got some real slow songs. Then we got some that are a little faster.

Tara: For me, the slowest songs tend to be grand entry songs, I guess because everybody has to dance to them. And then the fastest ones are the men's Fancy—real fast. Can you tell me anything about Traditional dancing, women's Traditional, and where it comes from?

Norma: The women's Traditional has been around for a long time. Pow-wows have been around for a long time. We got pow-wows in our Origin Stories that go way back and just during the dance the woman would dress in her best attire. And because the woman has connection with the earth, because the earth is our mother and they're both female, then that is why the woman Traditional dancer should be as graceful and use more of a swaying motion than a hopping motion. That's where that connection is, and that's how the women's Traditional Dance came about.

Tara: Did it used to be that women stood in one place, and it's changed now so they move?

Norma: We never do move. We stand still. There's so much controversy over some things. Some women turn to the right and then they'll go half-circle. And then some raise their fan and some don't.

Tara: On the honor beats?

Norma: On the honor beats, I don't turn. I don't know where that came about because they didn't used to a long time ago. They didn't turn. I think some Traditional dancers probably just tried to get a little fancier than standing still. So all they would do is turn, but they never turned in a full circle—never. And so I don't. I'm not quite sure when that came about. I know it was after the seventies, early seventies that the half-turn came into effect. But the raising of the fan on the four honor beats—that has always been. A long time ago a lot of people didn't have the eagle fan. Now everybody has the fan, but back then they didn't. Back then they raised their scarf. They'd hold a scarf, and they'd raise their scarf. And it was that raising of the scarf over your head on those four honor beats in honor of any veteran in your family whether it's a male or a female. It's in honor of every veteran who was willing to give their life for their people. And that was in any battle. So that includes Wounded Knee of '73. Somebody that was at Wounded Knee, that person was willing to give their life for the People. They are a veteran. Some people don't see them as veterans, but they are a veteran because they went to war against the United States government, and they were willing to give their life for their people. So those guys were honorable. I don't want to take away from the other veterans. But anybody that went in there knew they didn't have a chance. There were bazookas, there were tanks, there was everything out there. How could they have won? How could they have won a war like that? So to me, if a person had somebody at Wounded Knee of '73 they have a veteran in their family too. But I was always told it was the eldest child—eldest girl in each family—that had the right to raise their fan in honor of the veterans. But almost anybody can do that really. That's where the women's Traditional Dance came from.

Tara: Recently women have started to Grass dance, and I've heard that there are men up north, in fact, it's at Fort Peck, that are starting to dance as Jingle Dress dancers. Have you ever seen any women Grass dancers, and what do you think about that?

Norma: Again, I go back to the things my grandfather taught me. One is that he said, "It's okay when you're young." It's okay for a girl to Traditional or Grass [dance], and back then there weren't many Grass dancers. But he also said, "If they want to do it it's okay. But once they reach womanhood they start having their time, they're becoming a woman. Then they can't play like that." To him it was like playing—to the elderly then, that was playing, really. It's part of the role thing, and if you go outside the role it takes the power away. So I would say I'm all right with it clear up until that period in time, but after that I think we're sending mixed messages to our children. If we've got a man that's a Jingle Dress dancer, what are we saying to our young boys? "Oh, yeah, this is okay?" They can dress as a woman and dance, and it isn't okay. I don't feel it's okay. It's outside of the role that they should be portraying. Some say then maybe they're *winkté* [acting as a woman]. Well maybe they are and maybe they aren't. But it appears to be that they are. But even a long time ago if there was someone in the camp that was like that they still had respect for that person. They never disrespected a human being. That winkté also had a role. And they had to present themselves appropriately in public. There were certain things which he could and could not do. That's just like if you're not a winkté, there are still certain things you can or you cannot do according to society. It's always been like that. I don't agree with that [male Jingle Dress dancers]. When they're young it's okay. After they've come to their manhood or womanhood, I don't think that should be in public.

TRADITIONAL WOMEN

Tara: When you're dancing in a grand entry, what are you trying to do with your footwork? What do you listen for with the music?

Norma: Since I'm a women's Traditional dancer, it's a closeness with the earth, who is our mother. And so a women's Traditional dancer, her feet should never leave the ground. That's why they don't have a lot of fancy footwork. And their heels should always be together—of course, not as you're coming in grand entry, because you wouldn't be able to move. But when you're dancing—and that's part why the Northern women are stationary when they dance—when you're watching and judging a women's Traditional dancer, their heels should always be together, and the closer they are together, the better the dancer is. You watch for them to be on-beat. When that beat comes down, that dancer should be coming up. If that beat comes down and they're going down they're off-beat. The other thing is that they hold their head up and their fringe should be swinging the same way. Now I notice there's a lot of them where their fringe swings opposite. And then there's another style where they say that the fringe is dancing. So the fringe doesn't swing at all, it just kind of pops up at the bottom and dances.

Tara: I've seen them do like this [swing] with one arm.

Norma: Yes, that's opposite directions. Southern dancers do that when they're dancing. If you notice their fringe will go in an opposite direction. But the Northern dancers, their fringe should be going in the same way. That was what I was taught. But I see a lot of Northern where their fringe swings opposite, so maybe they were told something different. And I've even been told that may be a Cheyenne way, because it was a Cheyenne woman actually that said the fringe should be dancing. So it's probably hard to judge because we've got intertribal pow-wows, and different people have their different ways. So pretty much where the fringe is concerned you just go with whatever is your opinion.

Robert Rendon

SONG-MAKING AND PERFORMANCE

Robert: I started singing about six years ago with a Drum group called Denver Dakota from Denver, Colorado. And since then I sang with Pass Creek of South Dakota. I'm currently singing with Fly-In Eagle of Saskatchewan, Canada, and a Drum group me and some of my friends have in Denver called Eagle Plume.

Tara: Are you the head singer with the Drum or are you just . . . ?

Robert: Well . . .

Tara: What do you do with the Drum?

Robert: A lot of Drums have one certain head singer, but on our Drum group [Eagle Plume] we just more or less try to have everybody have a say-so in what goes on. There's no head guy.

Tara: Do you guys practice, and how do you do that?

Robert: Yeah, we practice twice a week. And we just basically go through our songs. Our Drum group has a lot of songs we've all helped make. Those are the songs we practice, and we try to sing only our songs at pow-wows. And occasionally we do sing other people's songs.

Tara: Do you compose or make songs yourself?

Robert: I've made four songs myself. The songs that I've made are all straight songs. Word songs are really hard to make 'cause they have to have a lot of meaning to them, but just straight songs are pretty easy to make.

Tara: How do you go about learning a song? What's the process of learning a song?

Robert: First you sit down and learn the words and what they mean. And then after you learn the words and what they mean, then you go into saying the words in the rhythm of the song.

Tara: Can you give me an example—just a short example—of just speaking the words to the song? How you would do that?

Robert: If it said, *Lakota oyate* and then *wacipi*, that would be "Lakota people dancing." Then we would just say that. But in the song they won't see it as straight plain-out—sometimes they change the way you say the words in a song, depending on how the rhythm goes.

Tara: What's the difference between, say, a song for a Fancy Dance contest and a song for a Grass Dance contest? Do you have certain songs that go to certain things?

Robert: Yeah, that's the whole purpose for words in straight songs. Certain word songs are only sung for certain things, depending on if it was a song made for women or if it was made for men. And then also the speed—the speediness of the song compared to your Traditional or Fancy Dance. Straight songs can pretty much be sung for anything, and that's just judged upon by the singers on whether or not they want to sing for that certain category, that certain song. There are some honor songs that are straight songs that are only to be sung for honor songs. But very rarely do you find a honor songs that are straight—most of them have words in them.

Tara: Can you sing for me a song that you've made? You feel comfortable doing that? Or singing anything for me?

Robert: What's it gonna be used for?

Tara: I won't put it out on a tape or play it for other people, but I might write it out.

Robert: Oh.

Tara: What I've noticed when I listen to songs is that they're constructed or put together a certain a way. With rounds and push-ups and things like that. So you'll have some words, and then there'll be a part where they'll say "hey-yayayayayayayaya-oh" or "hey-yayayayayaya-o-oi."

Robert: They're vocables, yeah.

Tara: But the song—I guess to me it has different sections. There'll be vocables, and then there'll be a part at the end where the rhythm simply will say "da-da-da-da-da-da." There is this song on the Pass Creek tape like this: "ya-dada-dada da dada dada-da" [then faster and tapping]. Like that, with these little ending sections?

Robert: At the end?

Tara: Yeah. Do you have names for those parts of the song, or do you have names for any parts of the song?

Robert: Not really. Well, in a song with one verse—you sing the part and then you pause. There's a short pause. The Drum keeps going, and then you sing that part over again. Then they have what's called a lead after you sing that part twice. There is someone that comes in and sings a solo-type of lead.

Tara: And takes it back to the top?

Robert: And then the rest of the Drum group backs 'em up with the same thing, and then they get back into what you would call the chorus or whatever.

Tara: What I've noticed with songs is there's a top part where it starts out, where you have usually the head singer, and then the second, and then they'll be singing a little bit. And then there are these different parts,

I call them "cadential patterns." They're these little parts that break up a song. What I've done is transcribe a bunch of these songs. Take them down [draws a diagram]. And I've noticed that they have a pattern. There'll be a part that will start here. You'll be the head singer. Then the second will come in. And then they'll be a little formula right there where they'll say something like "hey ya ho-yi ya." And then you go into the second part here where it'll just repeat. And then there are those little breakup parts where they go "hey-ya hoya hey yayayayaya-hey" or whatever [taps out the rhythm]. And there are specific little ones [cadences] I found out, especially with Lakota songs. These specific patterns of vocables where the singing will be like "da—da—da," and then everything will speed up. It'll get more intense. It'll be "dadadadadadadada."

Robert: That just goes in part with the song. There's a lot of songs that do that, and there's some that don't, that stay the same pretty much all the way through. I can sing you one of the songs I made, and then you can tell me if, if it . . .

Tara: If it works that way or not?

Robert: But it's not a word song.

Tara: Okay.

Robert: It's a Straight song. [Sings.] (The form of music example 9 is consistent on a basic level with that of the Great Plains Traditional style detailed in figure 3. Robert's song is unavailable in a recorded audio format.)

Tara: Yeah, that part you did at the end. The [sings the cadence].

Robert: Yeah, that's just like a "yea-ah." Where they drag it like that? That's just more or less the way they end songs. It's just an easier way of ending it. And then the rest of the Drum group backs 'em up with the same thing, and then they get back into what you would call chorus.

Tara: Now the honor beats, are they in a specific place in the song?

Robert: It's kind of like driving a car where you have to shift. [They are] usually on the second and fourth [push-up]. Just on the second one the honor beats will kind of bring the pace up. And on the fourth one the honor beats will bring the pace down. So the first push-up is normally kind of slow or medium, and then you come to your second push-up and the honor beats pick it up, and then you'll have your third push-up where it's at that level where you've brought it up to, and then your fourth push-up you'll bring it down.

Tara: What about the beat tempo with songs? I know some songs will start slow and then they'll speed up and some will be the same all the way through.

Robert: That's again just depending on the category you get—like

Music example 9. Straight Song by Robert Rendon (Oglala Lakota)

Fancy dancing or Traditional. Woman's Traditional normally isn't supposed to be fast. It's slow all the way through.

TOGETHER AROUND THE DRUM

Tara: How do you guys decide what pow-wows to go to? And how do things work out once you get to the pow-wow?

Robert: Most of the time it's a geographical thing, depending on how close it is and how much time we can get off work. And then once we get there, it's just pretty much on the pow-wow committee on how we sing and what we sing.

Tara: Okay, so you just pretty much go there, and you sit down and get ready, and they . . .

Robert: And they tell you what types of songs to sing.

Tara: How many singers are there in Eagle Plume? And how do you meet other singers? How do you find other people who like to sing and form Drum groups?

Robert: Usually if you're interested in the singing and you know a lot of songs, usually you can go and sit down at a Drum group. And usually they'll accept you in, and you sit and sing. It's just basically friends. Most of the Drum groups that get together are all friends or relatives that are all from the same reservation. But in our Drum group—just because there aren't too many people in Denver that are interested in singing—we have five [members] in Denver. Five, as our main singers. And then usually when we go to other pow-wows, there're friends of ours that we know who sing, and they know we sing. So they usually just jump in with us.

Tara: Some Drum groups are considered better than others, and some singers are considered better than others. What makes a good Drum group, and what makes a good singer?

Robert: A good singer would be someone that could sing real clear. A long time ago, singers, they sung at a different [pitch] level. They sung at a lower level. Nowadays, you find a lot of singers singing real high-pitched just because it's the trend, so that's what they consider the "good singer." The singer that can sing the highest, the loudest, the clearest, and the longest. People that can sing really long without frying out—their voices giving out on them. Someone who knows a lot of songs and knows what the songs mean.

Tara: What makes up a Drum group—that makes it a good drum group?

Robert: What makes up a Drum group? You gotta have a lot of respect. There are certain things you do and certain things you don't do. Like with the drum, you don't set things on the drum. You're not supposed to set things on the drum. You don't leave your drum unattended, by itself. If you do—and I've seen pow-pows where they do do this—a whistle-carrier can go blow the whistle on the drum if no one is sitting there. When someone blows a whistle, you're supposed to start singing. So if someone goes and blows a whistle on a drum and no one's around, they have the right to take that drum. So you're not supposed to leave your drum. I've been told people have different feelings about it, but women aren't supposed to sit around the drum. They sit behind the men, they stand behind the men and sing. They're not supposed to sit at the drum and sing. But through modernization and stuff you see it a lot.

Tara: What makes somebody a bad singer?

Robert: Makes 'em a bad singer?

Tara: Yeah. There are people who might start heading toward your drum, like they're going sit with you, and you're not sure if you want them there?

Robert: Yeah. There are people like that. I don't really know if I want to call them bad if it's just a case of inexperience. That or they're just learning. When you first learn, obviously, you're gonna be off-key. You're gonna be off-drum—you're not gonna be right-on. Because there are some songs that go really fast, and they won't be able to keep up with it, just because they're learning and they haven't learned yet. They haven't mastered the art yet.

Tara: Where do you get the drums?

Robert: We just have people make them. There are certain people that make drums, and you ask them to make 'em, and they make 'em for you.

Tara: Sometimes I see people using old high school marching-band drums.

Robert: Oh, yeah.

Tara: Do people use those any more?

Robert: That's a real old style of drum that they used to use. There are people that still do—we have one like that. But we took off the plastic head they had on there before and put a hide on it. But we have the actual, the drum part.

Tara: The shell of the drum part?

Robert: The shell.

Tara: What kind of hide is best?

Robert: Cow's really not that good. But it just depends on how high a pitch you want on your drum. Different hides like elk, or buffalo, or deer, they all come with a different pitch because of the thickness of the hide.

Tara: Is there any relationship between the pitch of the drum or the sound of the drum and how high the singers sing?

Robert: If the drum's high, naturally, you're gonna sing high just to match the drum. Because otherwise it sounds off. If the drum's low, you'll still have your highs, but you'll have a few of the guys in the Drum group that'll sing low just to keep in tune with the drum. Otherwise your sound will be off.

Tara: I know—because I play the drums myself—when you're outdoors and it's a day that's wet, the head is a little looser.

Robert: Yeah, it gets real loose.

Tara: Do you guys sing lower to match up with that head or do you take blow-dryers?

Robert: We take blow-dryers and heat it up. Either that or put it in a car and turn the heater on. We try to keep them to our voices.

Tara: So if you sit with somebody else's drum, do you change the way you sing a little bit to match their drum then?

Robert: Yeah.

Tara: So you have to be fairly versatile if you're going to go around to a bunch of different drums.

Robert: That's right. And that's how you can tell a good singer, too, is if they can do that. You don't want to jump on somebody else's Drum group and sing totally different than them—they're gonna hear you. You'll be off-key, and then you ruin their song. They're not gonna want you to sing with them anymore.

Tara: One more thing. How would dancers compete with the Drums? Are Drums allowed to do things, sort of like trick things [during competition]?

Robert: Normally they will ask for a trick song if they want it to be that way. Because otherwise a Drum group could just stop it and . . .

Tara: . . . do whatever they wanted?

Robert: Yeah. We have to stay within certain boundaries. Because there are certain songs made certain ways, and you got to sing them that way. And then the dancers will learn the song, and then, once they master that song, you make another song to see if they can get it.

DANCING

Tara: A long time ago you used to Grass dance. And then you started doing Traditional dancing. Do you still dance?

Robert: No I don't.

Tara: You don't, really?

Robert: Nope.

Tara: You're just a professional singer?

Robert: Yup. Well, no, I just don't know. Probably most of it is part out of laziness and just not getting the money together to get the outfit together. I still have all my feathers and stuff. I just need to get my beadwork and all that other stuff together. And it's kind of expensive.

Tara: You don't like your old outfit?

Robert: I grew out of it is what it was. I grew like six inches in one summer, so I grew out of it and just never got around to making another one.

Tara: That, I guess, happens. I've seen people with tapes actually practicing footwork to go with specific things happening in a song. Did you ever do that when you were Traditional dancing?

Robert: Yeah, you practiced moves. And that's just to impress the judges.

Tara: So would it be easier for you if during the competition a song that came up that you knew and you'd practiced?

Robert: Not so much that I knew. Some groups you can really get into just because some groups that go out there—some groups sound more enthused than others and that helps you a lot and the way you dance and how well you dance. You get into it more when the singers get into it more.

Tara: Do you think little Ardie is ever going to sing?

Robert: Oh, yeah, he's always running around singing.

Tara: Didn't he used to sit in your lap?

Robert: Yeah.

Tara: Norma would say, "Did you sit in his [Robert's] lap?" And he'd say, "Uh-huh."

Robert: When he's around at the pow-wows when I sing I usually try to have him sit with me. That's how it was when I was younger. Guys would have me sit with them just to keep it going with the younger generations.

Tara: Do you speak Lakota at all?

Robert: Not real well, but I can understand a lot of it.

Tara: So you can sing it pretty well.

Robert: I can because a lot of the songs have a lot of the same words. They just sung them different ways. I can understand the language pretty well, but when it comes to speaking it, singing is about all I can do.

On March 31, 2000, while traveling from Porcupine to Denver to celebrate Robert's birthday, Norma, Nadine, and Ardie Junior were hit from behind by a large commercial truck rig. The truck pushed the car for more than a mile down Interstate 80 at a speed of about seventy miles an hour. By the time the truck stopped, the back of the car was completely crushed and its frame had buckled. Although Nadine and Ardie emerged relatively unscathed, Norma was seriously injured, and her future as a pow-wow dancer is in doubt.

15. Amos Little (Iron Hawk), ca. 1901–2. Little was performing with Buffalo
Bill Cody's Wild West Show. Gertrude Käsabier photograph, courtesy of
Norma Rendon.

16. Wallace Little, Norma Rendon's grandfather. The floral-patterned beadwork on his vest, although typically associated with woodlands tribes, are also a long-standing tradition among the Lakota. Courtesy of Norma Rendon.

17. Norma Rendon in women's Traditional regalia. Courtesy of Norma Rendon.

18. Norma and Robert Rendon with Norma's
youngest son, Ardie Janis, Jr. Courtesy of
Norma Rendon.

19. Aspen Rendon Fancy dancing at the Oglala Nation Pow-wow, Pine Ridge, S.D. Courtesy of Norma Rendon.

20. Robert Rendon performing in the men's Northern Traditional Dance competition at the Oglala Nation. Courtesy of Norma Rendon.

21. Left to right: Tonya Little with Robert, Norma, and Aspen Rendon.
Courtesy of Norma Rendon.

22. George Martin in men's Northern Traditional regalia at the Ann Arbor Pow-wow, 1998. Photograph by the author.

23. Sydney Martin tends the store, Ann Arbor Pow-wow, 1998. Photograph by the author.

24. Left to right: David Shananaquet and Jeff Martin with the Skin Tones at the 1998 Ann Arbor Pow-wow. Photograph by the author.

25. Shannon Martin (left) with friend Gina Volare at the University of Michigan, Flint, Pow-wow, 1997. Photograph by the author.

7 *The Musical Life of an Anishnaabeg Family: Nda Maamawigaai (Together we dance)*

And it's just us, that's the way we are. We're supposed to dance—we were born to dance. Or to sing, or to drum, to make that traditional music.

—Sydney Martin

The Martins and Shananaquets are typical of many Anishnaabeg family groups in the Great Lakes region. George Martin (Ojibwe), now retired, served in the Korean War and worked for many years in the Michigan auto industry. His wife Syd (Potawatomi, photograph 23) works as a counselor, and they live near Hopkins, Michigan, in a house next to the Rabbit River. The area is near the old Salem Indian township, where Syd's family has lived for generations. David Shananaquet (Ottawa, photograph 24) and Punkin Shananaquet (George and Syd's middle daughter) live together with their two children, Carly and Paul, in a small house next to Punkin's parents, and David works nearby doing specialty painting at a custom furniture shop. He is also an accomplished artist and does a thriving business selling Indian-themed T-shirts and sweatshirts at pow-wows.

Shannon Martin (George and Syd's youngest daughter) is an engineering graduate of the University of Michigan (photograph 25). She lives in Ann Arbor and has worked for the university as a liaison between the campus Indian community and the university administration. Among

Shannon's responsibilities were planning and coordinating events for Native American Month (November) and the Ann Arbor Pow-wow, held every year on the third weekend in March.

All of the Martins, including Punkin Shananaquet and her two children, are active dancers on the Great Lakes pow-wow circuit, and David is a member of the Skin Tones Drum group. In addition to their public musical life, the family is active in the Three Fires (known also as the Midewiwin [Heartway]) Lodge. The *midé* movement is grounded in the original teachings, ceremonies, and prophecies of the Anishnaabeg, and participation in seasonal ceremonies strengthens and spiritually renews lodge members. Midé ceremonies hold the Native community together through shared beliefs, and their continuance assures the survival of the Anishnaabeg language and unique way of life.

In September 1997, the Martins and Shananaquets came together over three days for a series of conversations with me about the place of music and dance in their lives. We talked in a variety of settings: at an all-you-can-eat Chinese restaurant in Flint (day one) and their home in Hopkins (day two) and, for the interview with Shannon on day three, in my Ann Arbor hotel room. As in the interviews with the Rendons, I used a series of general questions and topics but had no definitive framework for controlling and ordering the conversations. Instead, each person chose their own topics, which reflected their interests and what they wished others to know about their pow-wow experiences. Other than editing out the "you knows" and a few sensitive references, their words—and mine—are presented as spoken. Syd Martin was very specific about that. "We don't speak the 'King's English,'" she stated, "but we aren't ignorant people either. It's important to be honest, so use just what we said."

Day One

POW-WOW HISTORY IN MICHIGAN

Syd: I'm from the Huron band of Potawatomi, and [my] traditional name is Ogemakwe, which means "Chief Woman." My clan is the Wolf Clan. My earliest memory of being at a pow-wow or out in public doing Indian things was with my mother (and although I say my mother, she's not my biological mother, because my real mother gave me to her first cousin—my adoptive mother—who had also raised her). She was a single lady in her mid-forties, and she was a basketmaker.

And so we went to the Greenville Michigan Centennial right before I started kindergarten. Our school was a little one-room schoolhouse that we lived by in our Indian settlement, which is called Salem. We were getting ready to go to the Greenville Centennial, which is near Grand Rapids. My mother loaded up all of her black-ash splints—they were like in a blanket, and they were all jumbled. And so she made me a little outfit for that [the Centennial]. It was not beaded or anything, but it had a lot of zigzags, and I was really proud of that because it was my first Indian clothes. And we were going to Greenville, and we were gonna be Indians. Mom made herself one, too, and we were in the Centennial parade.

And just because it was right before kindergarten starting, I had my hair cut. I used to have really long hair, like my daughter Shannon, who has lush, long, black hair. I had it cut and permed, my aunt gave me a Toni home perm and a cut—they would call those "poodle cuts" I think. So I was very proud to be an Indian girl going to Greenville to be an Indian and be in the parade. Eli Thomas was going to be there, and he brought his hand drum. When he would drum and then we would all dance around him, and do our Indian dances. And that was my earliest recollection of being in public and being with other Indian people.

From Greenville, we liked what we did as a group and with Eli Thomas, who is Chief Little Elk from Mount Pleasant. And he was always doing this in schools by himself and taking his baskets and stories, he was a storyteller to the schools. So we started finally adding on to our little dance troops. Eli was getting booked into schools around where we lived, and he'd come stay like two, three weeks with us every year, and we would go to the schools. They would pay Eli, and then he would pay his helpers like me, and I think I got around 50 cents or something. And my mom was able to sell her baskets. Of course school kids didn't have very much money, but teachers would buy 'em, and if she could just sell two $3 baskets she thought that was good.

After that, Greenville, then I remembered going to these things, and Eli—Little Elk—he started having pageants. One weekend a year in Mount Pleasant. Right at the council grounds there. And we would always go there and help him do that. Then we started going up to other places, and we would put on regular little mini pow-wows. By this time we had a lot of dancers. Well, a lot meaning probably twenty to twenty-five. And I was doing that up until about age thirteen, when I went to a ceremonial. George, what do they call those, at Chapel Lake?

George: Pageants?

Syd: Pageants. Every night we would put on a three-hour pageant. And it was professionally done by Reverend James Crewes. It was called the Chapel Lake Ceremonials, and a lot of people went to that. That's where I first made Joe Marcus and Ted Lefthand and all the Sebastians,

Dorothy and Elmer and Joanne Sebastian-Morris, who was later to become our maid of honor when we got married. That's when pow-wows and ceremonials started coming back in Michigan.

Tara: When did pow-wows go underground?

Syd: I would say in the late 1800s. Through all the boarding school problems, through the twenties and thirties when they tried to beat the language out of us and tried to teach us how to farm and how to do meaningful work in the factories [laughs]. Cleaning rich people's houses and things like that. It just wasn't good to be an Indian for so long, especially sharing with other Indian people like we do now in the big pow-wows like at Ann Arbor and Chicago. Where it's to get together to not only socialize, make new friends and greet old friends again, but it's to show off! Especially the spring pow-wows. "Look what we've done this round." And everybody's coming out in spring and early summer with all their brand new stuff, and it's just fun. Because Indian people are kind of competitive. You know, if you're the best beadworker, or you're the best sewer, you're the best!

So even the traditional people are always still evolving. And they would have been. We're not stuck like in the Curtis photographs of a long time ago. Like a lot of the hobbyists—we have some friends who are hobbyists. They have to be just exactly like an 1860 photograph. The grass-roots real Indian Traditional dancers now, they don't look like that. You won't be able to tell what tribe they're from if you saw some of those things that they have. And plus, with the way we can motor around the country now, or fly around the country, we see other dancers, and we make other friends from far away. So we wear those with our dance clothes. A lot of our white hobbyist friends will say, "Well that's not Potawatomi, Sydney!" And I'll say, "But it's a gift from my relatives. I'm going to honor that by wearing it. I don't care if it isn't Potawatomi."

We know who the people who enjoy pow-wows are because they're wearing things that we know were gifts. They're not wearing things that are just made to be specifically for one tribe like in a museum, which is fine. We're not museum people! We're living, evolving, cultural people. And now that Michigan is finally beginning to be where communities are proud to be sponsoring and putting on pow-wows, and there are two and three pow-wows a weekend now. And it brings everybody out, not just the dancers. It's a community thing, where people come together to eat and visit and laugh and share and to have honor songs.

TRADITIONAL DANCING AND THE ROLE OF
THE VETERAN

George: I'm from Lynx Clan of the Ojibwe Nation, I'm originally from Lac Courte Oreilles Reservation in Wisconsin. One of the first memories of a pow-wow, when I first started dancing, is the Fourth of July. Every Fourth of July they would have a dance at Reserve—a town, a little village, called Reserve. We lived in the town of Whitefish—a little village of Whitefish. And we used to go there on the Fourth of July and we would have a pow-wow. I remember as a little boy growing up, the big drum was there and not very many dancers, but there was a lot of spectators. They had little pop stands out, and craft stands along the arena. And we had a Hoop dancer, who used to dance quite a bit. I remember the Jingle dresses back then. There was a couple ladies that had Jingle dresses. And we never danced. But later on they wanted dancers out at the fair, so one lady got together some kids, and they had their parents make little outfits for them, and so we went out to the fair and danced. That was the first time I ever danced. I was probably seven or eight years old.

I left the reservation when I was seventeen, and I never did return to it yet. I didn't want to go back for visits and all that. I went in the service for ten years, and I never did anything like pow-wows and or beadwork til I got out of the service in '64. And I then started dancing again—that's when I started dancing. And I've been dancing ever since then.

I'm a men's Traditional dancer. To explain that dance, to tell you about it, you have to go back a long way in time. You have to go back to the beginning of time of the Anishnaabeg people. Our elders teach us that when the Creator made the universe, after he made Mother Earth and after he made all these things on there—all these living things—they tell us that he wanted someone down here. Someone down here on this Mother Earth to live in harmony with these things that he created, to take care of them in a good way. And that is when they say that he created the Anishnaabeg man and lowered him down onto this Mother Earth. I know a lot of you know us as Indians or Native Americans. In our language we have our own names. We call ourselves Anishnaabeg. And that means the first man lowered onto this Mother Earth.

And as he was being lowered he could see the beauty in where he was going. He could see the forests and the rivers and the valleys. All these things he was seeing for the first time. And as he got closer to this Mother Earth he could the animals running in the woods. He could see the birds flying in the air, fish swimming in the water, and could see all the beautiful plants. And all these things he was seeing for the first time was things he was gonna take care of. And his first steps on this Mother Earth—very first steps—were so soft and gentle. So soft that he did not offend any grass on Mother Earth, because he was sent here to take care of that and not to harm it in any way. So he walked very gentle on Mother Earth, and that is the way that Traditional men dance today and Traditional women. They dance in that way. Very soft on Mother Earth.

And all these things on Mother Earth—the living things—he'd be taking care of them. Like the bear, the eagle, and the fox, wolf. All these things he was supposed to take care of. When Anishnaabeg first came down [the living things] made a promise that they would take care of us while we live on this Mother Earth. They told the Creator they would give us food to eat, clothes to wear, things to make our homes with. And today, today they still keep that promise that they made to the Creator thousands of years ago. When we dance, we dance in buckskins. Our bustles are made of eagle feathers, and our ropes are made of horsehair and have eagle feathers in them. We have bandoleers made of deer hooves, necklaces made of bear claws. And all these things that we use were given to us by them that we call our brothers and our sisters—our four-legged brothers. Because they told us that they would take care of us while we're here. And all these things that we wear, we have to take care of them in a good way. Because once we leave this Mother Earth, we can't take these things with us. And in our teachings we must teach our children some of these good ways and how to take care of these things that our brothers let us use. Which we dance in and put 'em away real good. We don't horde or get as many as we can. I only have one eagle-wing fan because that's all I can use is one. We have to use them and take care of them in a good way.

And it's Traditional dancers that are like storytellers, as we dance we tell stories of something that happened in our lifetime. Maybe a war story or a hunt or maybe something special in your life that you want other dancers or the people in the audience to know the story of.

The outfit that I wear is a men's Traditional outfit. And it's mostly based on the veteran. The roach that I wear is a veteran's roach, even the feathers that are in the roach are used only by veterans. The white spikes that we wear are taken from that piece. The bustle that is all the eagle feathers is part of the veterans. Veterans are in charge of all the feathers that are given or worn on regalia during the pow-wow. If a feather drops, the veteran takes care of that. Whenever you take a veteran's job you should know all these things that have to be done when things like that happen. The roach that I wear has red in it, that's how you know it's a veteran's roach. And I carry an eagle-wing fan and a tomahawk pipe. All these things that I wear are based on the veterans or have things to do with the veterans. I do have an eagle staff that I carry, that I use at pow-wows. I'm usually at a pow-wow every weekend. People or different committees ask to have a veteran to come in, and I'm usually asked to come in different places. I've been to Canada and all over Michigan. That's the outfit that I wear. I don't have to compete as a Traditional dancer—I very seldom contest. I don't go in for a lot of extra things on my outfit that I wear.

I'd like to talk now a little about the grand entry. As a veteran and as a head veteran at a lot of pow-wows, I think it's entirely up to the head veteran who they pick for their pow-wow. Some head veterans who are at pow-wows are not combat veterans and some are combat veterans. And the staff that we carry is very old. It is the oldest flag that we know of. And a long time ago, these veterans, these warriors that carried these staffs into battle were the first to go. The first one to meet the enemy with that staff and to bring that staff back again to have some strong, strong medicine. When the combat veteran carries that staff into the arena, he still has that medicine. No pictures should be taken because of the medicine that he has with him, the sacred things that he has. Even young children are not allowed to be in that color guard—they don't want children even close because of the medicines that might hurt them. It's not that we don't want the children around, but the medicines that they carry are very strong. It might hurt them, even in their lodges, the day lodges, we try to keep our children away, a certain distance to where these medicines will not hurt them. Because they are powerful medicines that they carry and to return from battle with that staff, we know that they had some strong medicine. And to carry it, to lead our people into an arena for a pow-wow, they still have that medicine, with a sacredness, and that's when I think it's up to the veteran himself—the head veteran—if he should have pictures taken or not.

Finally, I'd like to speak on the difference between a traditional and a contest pow-wow. Before I start explaining, I'd like to tell you that about four years ago I went out to Leech Lake in Minnesota. My wife and I, we went on a trip, just to go to different pow-wows. And we ended up in Leech Lake, Minnesota on a Monday morning. And they said that they were going to have a traditional dance, starting Wednesday. So we stayed there, and the people treated us real nice, real good. We felt like we belonged there, the way they treated us. They gave us food to eat and made sure that we were camped down good. When storms came in, they came and helped us with our tent. And on Wednesday, they started a traditional pow-wow, which we danced every day there. And we danced Wednesday, Thursday, and Friday in the traditional pow-wow. Then all of a sudden, all of these traditional people up and left. They tore up their camps and left, and then a new group came in. They said that "the contest people are coming in now. We're gonna have a contest pow-wow." But we stayed anyway, just to see them 'em, because we were camped out and that's what we came out there for.

So we stayed for the contest pow-wow. And these ones treated us the same way—real good and nice. We met some wonderful people there, even at the contest pow-wow, which lasted Friday night, Saturday, and Sunday. At that contest pow-wow, they started it probably at noon, and sometimes it wouldn't finish until 6 or 7 o'clock the next morning. Whereas at the traditional pow-wow, we wouldn't dance that long.

But this traditional pow-wow was really good. We met a lot of nice people, and they danced the traditional ways, and they had those naming ceremonies and feasts. But where the contest pow-wow came in, it was strictly dancing for, they danced for prizes, prize money. And you could tell the difference between the outfits that they wore. For the contest pow-wow, they came in with flashy outfits and with a lot of colors, a lot of feathers, whereas for the traditional there were a lot of old people who had no flashy outfits. And the contest pow-wow was where we all dance for that money. But it was still good. I still had good feelings there, but I guess that you could feel the difference between the traditional and the contest pow-wow when you experience something like that, real close, just going from traditional to contest, you can feel the difference. And that's not in a bad way.

DANCING, FAMILY, AND FRIENDS

Syd: I really admire my oldest daughter Punkin, because she says she's going to be the first woman in Michigan to bring back Grass dancing. She's a woman and she's going to build herself a Grass Dance outfit. She's already talked to our lodge chief, Eddie Benton, and what he said was that women were Grass dancers too, along with young boys, a long, long, long time ago. And that all of these things people say we can do and we can't do are European concepts and not ours. We didn't differentiate between jobs that a male could do and a woman couldn't do. I'm very proud of my four grown children now because they're all dancers. Jeff is in the army, but he still comes home once a year and spends thirty days. When we go to pow-wows he'll sing at the drum, and he's starting to build his traditional outfit to wear when he gets retired from the army in eight more years. He was a Fancy dancer in his day. Also, my grandchildren all dance—and that's very special. When we go to a little pow-wow or competition pow-wow we're all together—the three generations, doing these things.

The feel-good part about Traditional dancing is when you actually do hear the drums and you dance. It just takes away the worries—you don't have to think about what to make for supper next Tuesday, when you're going to go to some meeting, or what's going to go on. You just don't need to think about any of these things. The only thing that's important is that you're dancing now and you're feeling that inside your heart. And your feet are—your grandfather willing—your feet are willing to move to carry you around that circle. The best thing that could happen to anybody is to be able to do that. And that's what dancing is. Even though Traditional women aren't expressive [in dance movement], it is expressive to themselves in ways inside that nobody knows about. They're getting in tune with the feelings that they're having, and they're acknowledging something to themselves that nobody knows about.

It's just an honor to be able to live and to dance and to greet each day when you have these feelings that are right out in the forefront like that. I'd like to share that with everybody that I know and people that I don't know—if they can see me and say, "Gosh, what is she thinking about?" or "Why isn't she smiling when she's out there dancing? She doesn't look like she's having a very good time at all." If I could just make somebody stop a minute and think. Just to listen to that, to see what it feels like coming up to that drum. That's something that I wish I could leave for every human on our Mother Earth. *Miigwetch* [thank you].

Day Two

COMPARISONS

Tara: One thing that I was going to ask you about is when I was at Rosebud Fair [on the Lakota Reservation in South Dakota] what I noticed is that the men and women there dance in different directions. The men dance on the outside and they actually dance counterclockwise, and the women dance on the inside and they dance clockwise. And I was asking the women about that, because I hadn't seen it before. Is that something that you folks have heard of? Does everybody dance in the same direction? And why do people dance in the direction they dance in?

George: In our teachings, there's just one clan that dances in that direction, counterclockwise, and that's the Wolf Clan. They're the guardians of our lookouts.

Tara: When I was out at Rosebud, the pow-wow was really a fair, a big carnival and rodeo and pow-wow, and it was dusty, it was so dusty! Are there any Great Lakes pow-wows that are at all like that?

David: Probably the closest thing to something like that here would be the Michigan Festival, because we're off in our own little area. There's concerts and it's not really a carnival, but there are different bands playing. There're different areas of what's like a town, and parts where there's craft presentations, and a lot of different musics.

Tara: Is the Michigan Festival sort of a pow-wow?

David: No, this is put on by the state of Michigan. Michigan State University.

Tara: Are there any reservation pow-wows here that have carnivals?

Syd: I would think Mackinac, where we once did a dance—but they didn't have a carnival or have horses. They do have all the other things.

David: They'll have hockey games and basketball tournaments.

Tara: So there isn't any sort of prohibition against having that kind of stuff happening? I remember a weird little pow-wow about four or five years ago when I was still living here, and I remember they put you [George] on a horse!

Syd: Oh, that was in St. Claire. That was sort of a rodeo there. Yeah.

Tara: You didn't look totally comfortable on that horse. [Laughs.]

David: Yeah, and we did one in Detroit like that.

Syd: That was 'cause I wanted him [George] to be on the horse. Oh yes. [Laughs.]

Tara: I don't remember you on the horse, I remember him on the horse.

Syd: No, I wanted *him* to be on the horse. I thought it would be a good photo op! [Everyone laughs.]

David: Next rodeo calendar!

George: There's pow-wow that's like a carnival—I've never been there—but there's one in Milwaukee.

Syd: Summer Fest.

Tara: Oh, okay, Indian Summer Fest.

George: They have a carnival. I've never been there.

Tara: They got a lot of bingo there, too.

David: We've done presentations, though, not a pow-wow but presentations where there've been carnivals and stuff going on at the same time. It's not a regular pow-wow, though, it's just like we're doing a little show.

Tara: They have a lot of those kinds of things out in Los Angeles—we even have an Indian arts show in Santa Monica.

FANCY DANCING AND WOMEN'S ROLES

Tara [to Punkin]: You're a Fancy dancer, right?

Punkin: Yeah.

Tara: And you're still dancing. Can you say anything about being a Fancy dancer and how you got into it, and if you want to make any comments about the Grass Dance you can, or any other dance.

Punkin: I remember as a child, Fancy dancing and watching the actual woman's Traditional Dance style of dancing. I had a little skirt and a ribbon shirt and a shawl. And I was really caught up in wanting to do the boy's Traditional Dance, and I probably practiced it more. So my mom and dad made me a little boy's Traditional outfit, with the apron and the ropes, little beaded bustle trailers, and a little feather bustle. And so I became a little boy's Traditional dancer. I remember that being a good time—I liked dancing that style. I was glad I had the opportunity to have parents that gave me a choice, where I could have my dreams realized.

And as years went on, I'd seen the style of Fancy Shawl being brought into Michigan by Angie and Rae Bush, who are Frank Bush's daughters. Among other women there was Evelyn White Eye Williams, and Mary Lefthand, and they were such beautiful dancers in that style, so I became attracted to that Fancy Shawl style. And a few of my very good pow-wow friends: Becky and Ester, Becky Shalifoe and Ester Marcus. So we went through the same time, and we all became involved in dancing the Fancy Dance style. It was a lot of fun. To have friends that were starting out, watching the older women, too, they were very graceful and poised. We probably were some of the earlier Fancy dancers in Michigan.

Tara: Can you give me an approximate year of this?

Punkin: Say, probably from '69 to '73. Because the pow-wow, we became involved in the mid-sixties, so by the time I had become maybe ten or eleven I was more interested in the Fancy Shawl—grown out of my boy's outfit into the Shawl by then. But just watching that new wave of dance come across Michigan, the first time it was seen here—all the young women that wanted to dance the style.

Tara: Were there any women dancing Jingle Dress at all during this time?

Punkin: Yes, back when we had our Michigan pow-wows. And also I've heard that in Minnesota and Canada that style never really died. There were some elders of that dress who had kept that tradition alive. And my sister-in-law was probably one of the first Jingle-dressers in Michigan. She had learned that style.

Tara: What was her name?

Punkin: Katherine Gibson. David's sister is a Shananaquet also. And so she more or less brought it back here with many teachings about the dance.

David: Yeah, she got it the right way instead of—like a lot of these girls now—just picking it up and taking off with it. But out there she was presented with it and given it with the teachings.

Punkin: And a gift was given to the dress. And you know, every year or two when she makes a new dress, she always tries to have a gift for the dress. 'Cause that's the way she was taught out there.

Tara: Betty Pamp told me some things about Jingle Dress before I started dancing. She talked about 365 cones, and every day you sewed one cone onto the dress, and those sorts of things. And she also mentioned the berry fast. I didn't know what that was at the time, but then I learned she was talking about going on a berry fast. Is that something that you can talk about?

Punkin: One of my relatives had been on a berry fast for a year, and she gave up eating of blackberry, raspberry, blueberry, strawberry, and cranberry. She didn't eat any of those berries, all through the seasons. When she came out of her fast, her Aunt Monica made a dress for her to come out in, that was a Jingle dress with strawberries on it.

Tara: It's that one that I just saw?

Punkin: And so that's when she was welcomed into our womanhood roles and to our people. One of the roles that much younger women do and learn.

David: Kathy started her at about eight years old.

Punkin: After that ceremony there're a couple of young women in line that are involved in a berry fast themselves. We're aunts of this young woman now.

Syd: Someone there commented that this might be an equivalent to a debutante ball. Because we're presenting her to our society as a woman, and they should start treating her accordingly.

Punkin: It's so important for us to recognize our young people. In today's modern society they don't really get acknowledged.

AT THE DRUM

Tara: What's the name of your drum?

David: The Skin Tones. Our Drum, it's all family members.

Tara: I was talking to a friend out there [on Pine Ridge], we were talking about the whole issue of women at the drum, because there are some women who sit at the drum out there. But she said that that's a right that

you have to get from your family. And then I know that around here
women don't sit at the drum. I've heard there's a reason for that.

David: Right.

Tara: Is that anything you guys can talk about?

George: Here's the story I've heard. They say that the drum was giv-
en to the women, and they brought it back, she set it down and told the
men to sing at it. She'd stand back. That's what they do now.

Tara: The way that she was telling me the story was the women were
standing around the men.

George: To be sure they treat it right.

Tara [laughs]: It's an interesting situation out there. Everybody seems
to have a different tradition. Dave, here are some more questions. How
long have you been singing with the Drum? What got you going with it?

Dave: I got started probably the late seventies. My friend Moose Pamp
was the first one to bring me out to the drum. I was just sitting off—I was
off to the sidelines, and he asked me to come and sit down and join him.
I said, "Well I don't know what's going on." And he said, "That's why
you learn, just come over here and try to pay attention as best you can,
and you'll pick it up." I probably didn't join the Drum until maybe 1980,
1981. That was when my brother and brother-in-law got together and
decided we're going to start a Drum up.

It was rough going. We got laughed at and heckled because when
you're first starting out, you'll have big plans of tearing off with a song.
Then about half-way through you forget what you're singing. A lot of
times we'd pick up songs, but we really didn't know what they were for.
So you'd sing a song and it'd be the wrong type of song, and then one of
the elders or a different drummer would tell you that you made a mistake. You just have take it on the chin and roll with it and try not to do
it again—make the same mistake.

I been singing probably about seventeen years now, and I still feel like
there's a lot to learn. For a while there, I thought we were doing pretty
good, but then I see some of these groups from Saskatchewan, and these
guys just blow me away.

Tara: Do you compose or write your own songs?

Dave: Our group does, yeah. We'll write down different phrases, and
we'll give them to an aunt or a friend or elder that will translate it into
the Ottawa or the Ojibwe language.

Tara: So you start out with a written phrase in English?

Dave: Yeah, just to try to get what we want to say in English. Because
none of us are really fluent in the [Anishnaabeg] language. We all know

little bits and pieces, but we put it down in English, and then our aunt will translate it. She'll rewrite it into English what the phrase says, and once we do that, then we work on melodies to put with the words that they give us.

Tara: With pow-wow songs I know that there are certain things that make up the form of the song. You usually go through it a certain time, you have a certain number of repetitions, certain kinds of little phrases and vocal things you put at the end. Can you talk at all about how you think of a song in terms of how it's put together?

Dave: Myself, I'm more into like the music part of it, the melody. My brother and my brother-in-law, they're more into the words. I don't know, I guess I'm not an expert on . . .

Tara: You just sing it?

Dave: When we're making a song I don't pay attention to the words at all. They take care of that. I like the melodies. That's, if there's like a pretty melody then I get a better feeling, and then the words come later. I guess when you're making up a song you work on your melody, then you try to put your words in. Sometimes you put them in the beginning, sometimes you put them in the end. Wherever it works best.

Punkin: There are some people that are really gifted with they can just sit somewhere and they can make a song up that sounds beautiful. And then there are some people that just need to hear it over and over . . .

Tara: Repeated?

Dave and Punkin: Yeah.

Tara: Repetition?

Punkin: Repetition. Some are just naturally gifted at making a song. It's hard to explain.

(Music example 10 is a Skin Tones Traditional song that follows closely the Great Lakes Traditional form [fig. 3]. The text of the song, "Ambe giiwedaa aazigo wiisinidaa," translates as "let's go home now, and we will all eat." A few vocables are interspersed between the words of the Ojibwe text to make the melodic line smoother and easier to sing.)

Dave: We have a friend—Harvey Preeber—he's the lead singer of the Whitefish Juniors, and he's been singing with our group the past year. And he amazes me because, like between the songs that we sing, he'll be sitting there humming melodies. He'll come up with new songs just while he's sitting there. But he's fluent at his language [Ojibwe], too, so that really helps him out. I'll sit there and I'll listen to him, and he'll just start out his little hum and then keep going on it. Then he'll ask for the tape player and put it on the tape for us, and it's a new song. My brother's like that, too, he can come up with melodies off the top of his head.

Music example 10. Traditional Song by the Skin Tones (Anishnaabeg)

Punkin: There're also drummers that can hear a song once and then they know what it is and they keep it in their brain.

Tara: Yeah, I've known people like that . . .

Dave: Paul's [his son] like that.

Punkin: They know many songs.

Dave: He's one of my songkeepers, Paul is.

Tara: Some people that have that gift. Now here's something that Norma [Rendon] was talking about, which was interesting. She was talking about the tempo, or the speed of music in terms of beats. She was talking about music being a beat ahead, half a beat ahead as something you'd want to sing. And what she was talking about was, she said, "Okay, here is Pine Ridge, our beat, it sounds like [tap tap tap tap tap at 130 beats per minute]." And farther up north it's about [seven taps, slightly faster]. She described that difference as being half a beat faster. So she's thinking of the songs in terms of beats. Is that something that you folks do or have heard of?

David: I don't know, I guess it depends on what kind of song that we're singing. If we're singing a women's Traditional, you tend to slow things down to more of a heartbeat rate or somewhere in that neighborhood, and probably the same for a slow start in the Grass Dance. For the Fancy dancers we try to speed up. Also, if we're going to have words in our songs then we try to match the beat up so everything comes out smooth and it's not broken and choppy. One helps the other—that's kind of the way we try to take it. Even with the chant, we try to make the vocables, we try to keep it so everything has a flow to it. Some Drums sound a little choppy—their beat, their chant, are going at the same time. We try to get it so it's close.

Tara: When you do use words to talk about how fast something is, do you use the terms just "fast beat," "slow beat," "medium beat"? What sort of vocabulary do you use?

David: Yeah, we'll just say, "We'll start off with it in a medium beat." That's . . .

Tara: And this is where it gets interesting. Can you clap sort of a medium beat?

David: A medium beat would probably be like [claps at 130 beats per minute].

Tara: And a slower beat?

David: A slower beat would be [claps at 120 beats per minute]. That would be more to like a woman's Traditional to start with. Like an honor song, you want to start those out kind of slow.

Tara: How about give a Fancy Dance beat?

David: For a Fancy Dance for when we do our programs, we'd start out with a medium-fast beat, probably like [claps at 142 beats per minute] and keep that up through maybe three times through the song and bring it up on the fourth time through [claps at 186 beats per minute]. Then I get chewed out at the end of the day!

Tara [laughs]: Do you ever do things when you see dancers? I actually saw, at a pow-wow in Wisconsin once, there was this one Fancy dancer out there, and he was very strange, and the Drum seemed to be doing this on purpose, making him fall apart. Is that the kind of thing that you guys ever . . .

David: Oh, yeah, we kind of do battle with dancers out there. It depends on what kind of dancers are out there. Just to have fun, we'll throw in different stuff or a different beat on them and try to mess them up a little bit [laughs]. But most of it's just for fun.

Tara: Some of what I wrote here [on the question list] are thoughts about the drum style and attitudes toward the instrument. I've talked to people out west who consider their drum to be a living entity—the drum has a name. People give offerings to the drum. I've seen where the drum is given a eagle feather and things like that. How do you folks feel toward the drums?

Dave: I have my own drum, and I try to take care of it. I keep it wrapped up in a blanket, and we have a feast for it probably a couple of times a year now. It doesn't have a name, but as far as an Indian name, call it "Skin Tone Drum." I was going to get an Indian name for it, but everyone seems to like the name that I have now. My brother-in-law has a drum that we use too in our group, and he got his drum named—got an Indian name for it. So we use both drums. Depends on where we're going and who has to travel further. We never leave the drum unattended, make sure somebody's taking care of it at all times, you know, if there's not then we put it up and put it away.

Punkin: Little kids know not to go running through and pounding on the drums.

Dave: When we first started out we got into a lot of trouble because we'd leave our drums unattended. And from some of the elders, we got cussed out for it. Plus some of the things we were doing when we were leaving the drum—we'd go out to the car and have a beer or something. We were just young so we didn't know what we were doing. We've learned a lot of things over the last fifteen years or so. So we try to be more at the drum, we try to be more respectful. Keep the area clean. Before we'd throw a blanket over it, people'd be eating on it and stuff like that [laughs]. Just using it for a table. That stuff doesn't happen any more.

Tara: This will be under anonymous!

Dave: When you're first starting out you don't know these things—we didn't. We just were going to start a Drum. I guess you could say we didn't go through the proper channels. We just thought it'd be a cool thing to do, so we did it [laughs]. But we didn't know the protocol that you're supposed to have, so you learn that as you're going along. Like my son now, he started when he was small, so he knows—he was raised with it.

Tara: Does he sing too?

Dave: Oh yeah. He's going through his voice change now, but he's one of our lead singers, so he's a little gun-shy right now. His voice is changing. But he's the one that comes up with a lot of our songs for us that we sing. He's got something like a memory bank! Paul [his son], he keeps a lot of our songs. He knows what songs go to which dances. Punkin and I, we decide when they're going to dance. I started bringing him to the drum when he was eight years old, and he just took to it. By the time he was maybe eleven years old he was making songs up for us. And he did that for probably three years. He was one of our lead singers. Then his voice started changing, so he's laying off it right now. But we're trying to get him back, because his voice seems to be pretty strong now. Myself and his uncles, we're trying to prod him to get back going again, don't be scared. He's afraid because it's a little squeaky once in a while.

Tara: Let me ask Punkin a question that just came into my head. Since you're a dancer, when you dance, do you try to fit your footwork at all to what's happening with the music?

Punkin: Right. I try to, if the song is really good. There are a few Drums that—whether it's them singing or if it's the drum [instrument] itself—bring out a little inner step in me. If it's a song that's sung really good, if it has a really good melody and the beat is not dragging, I can almost flow with that song intuitively. But there are some Drums that aren't that good—I'm not trying to put a Drum down, they're trying—but they're not up to that par of doing what the dancer's style wants to do. So you really have to work at it when you're dancing to a bad drum. It's more work to dance. Whereas if you're dancing to a good drum with a good beat, it's effortless. The song can carry you. You kind of get an inner strength. Because I'm getting older, it takes a lot to dance this Fancy Dance style. So the better the Drum and if it's nice and smooth [i.e., the singing], I can really still put it into gear with those types of Drums.

But I do a lot more of the footwork. A lot more younger dancers are getting more into the athletic part of the dance. More of the spinning and how fast you can spin. But I've been complemented a couple of times for preserving that old style of Shawl Dance, which is just a lot of gracefulness and a lot of poise. Maybe a little bit of attitude thrown in.

But all that does come into play. You're dancing your style. Having a good attitude—whether it's mean or a type of a kick-ass type of an attitude—you still have to carry your strength out into that dance circle with you. And that's like the dance—how they do in the ballet. It's your inner strength that sometimes lets you make it through the song. But it's good, a nice feeling to be out there dancing.

(While Punkin, David, and I were talking, George sat, quiet as he drew. At the end our our conversation he handed me a diagram of powwow spatial relationships [fig. 10b].)

Day Three

BEING THE YOUNGEST

Shannon: I'm Ojibwe and Potawatomi, from the Lynx Clan. I'm twenty-seven years old. I've probably been dancing since I could walk—and even before that! I would be on a cradleboard, my mom and dad would carry me around on a cradleboard to their little dance presentations and programs and to little pow-wows here and there. So as soon as my feet probably hit the ground, off and running, I was dancing. Being that young, being raised traditionally and being around the drum and the music and the people, you learn from that by looking. And observing and watching. So I probably picked up a lot of my little moves by watching the adults. When you're that little you're clumsy and fumbly anyway, so you're really not dancing on beat to the drum. That takes time, and getting older, and practice. I started out as a little [Fancy] Shawl dancer. Being that small you don't really have a lot of possessions on your outfit because you do more running around with your friends at the gatherings than you do out being in an arena, but I did dance a lot. So my outfit was a little shawl—it was purple and blue and green, and my older sister and my mom made it for me. So I had my little shawl and then I had my little ribbon shirt, my skirt, and my moccasins and at that time they were lace-up moccasin boots. So they were all one piece. They wrapped around your leg and you tied them. And I think I had a little turquoise ring on, and when I would dance I'd take the turquoise ring off and put it on a scarf.

That was my outfit. And I never really had my hair done. At that age, my hair was cut in a Florence Brady—they call it a Florence Henderson—a shag cut.

Tara: Like the Brady Bunch?

Shannon: Yeah. Because when I was that young, I didn't like to get my hair washed or have it combed or cared for. I just liked to run around. And it was sticky and dirty and smelly. But I was happy, and my mom and dad would always try to wash my hair and I'd put up a fight about it. My grandma would always say, "Oh just leave her be. She's fine." Before I went into kindergarten, and first grade, both years I had to get my hair cut from the summertime. Because they said, "You're not taking care of your hair, we have to cut it a little bit, and make sure it's manageable and you can look presentable." So I didn't have any hair-ties or anything in my hair. Just my shawl, my ribbon shirt, my skirt, and my moccasins and my scarf. So that was basically my first outfit.

And I would contest and get [win] tiny tots, and then I eventually got up to the six-to-twelve-year-old dance category style. At that time I really began to take dancing seriously. I would be up there most every intertribal, spinning around. I've been told that there are home movies of me dancing when I was that young.

So as I got a little bit older, seven, eight, nine years old, I began to really take my dancing seriously. And that's when I went to my older sister, Punkin, and said, "Can you teach me some moves and practice with me so that I can stay on beat with the drum?" And then I can hear the drumbeat and the song and I can know when honor beats are coming up and when the song is going to stop. Because prior to that it was guesswork. Being that young, you don't always know when the song is going to stop. You keep on dancing and twirling even after the drum ends, and that's not counted when you're at a pow-wow and at a contest. So around that age I began to really take my dancing seriously and practice between pow-wows, which was during the weekdays. And Punkin would take me outside and we'd get the old boom-box going, and she would show me dance moves and spins. And we would dance in the different styles. We would put on the regular pow-wow intertribal songs, then we would do Crow Hops, and we would do Round Dances.

As time went on, I really began to dance and practice. And when you do that, older people take notice of you. That you're going to the pow-wows, you're not running around loose, and your parents know where you are, and you're in that arena. And you're dancing in that circle with the people. The elders take notice of that, and the older people.

And one time, I remember—I don't know where we were at—but this woman from Walpole Island gave me a full set of beadwork. Which included hair-ties, a choker, barrettes, and a belt. And that was a great honor to have somebody single you out and say, "You're a good little dancer, you need some more beadwork. You need to build up your—start building up your—outfit, and I want to help you." So that was my beadwork that I had from that woman. And that's what I wore for probably two or three years. Until the time when my family and I went to Chicago Pow-wow and our van was broken into and all our outfits were stolen.

Tara: Oh, I didn't hear about that.

Shannon: Yeah. We were in a parking garage. And it was big for us, from little Hopkins, Grand Rapids, to save up our money. Pile in the red truck, you know, my grandmother, my three siblings, and my mom and dad, to go to Chicago Pow-wow. And actually it was, we had the van then. And all of our stuff, every single outfit was stolen.

Tara: Can you give me a year for that?

Shannon: I think that was right around 1977. Somewhere right around in there. My older sister Punkin, my brother Jeff, and my other older sister Chip, me, and my mom and dad. All our outfits were taken out of our van, and my dad's CB radio, the Pendleton blankets that we had in there. The only thing that they left behind was my grandma's baskets and splints. My grandma carried that stuff around in garbage bags. So they probably didn't see them as much value, or probably they were just scrambling around taking things, they didn't look into the garbage bags. So those things remained in the van. But that was pretty distressful for us. Because that was our way of life, and our coming together every weekend was to dance together at pow-wows. So it took a while for us to build up our outfits again. At that pow-wow [Chicago], people found out about us, they held an honor song for us—a Blanket Dance. And we were given some money to begin buying beads and buckskin and stuff to get our outfits together again. Some people came who gave us some shells and cones. People gave us gifts like that, so you could tell how heartbreaking it was not only for us but the whole community knowing that we were a pow-wow family and this had happened to us. So with that went my outfit from my beadwork that a woman had given me.

My next outfit was actually hand-me-down from Punkin. She gave me her yellow beadwork. And I wore that way up until I was probably fifteen, when Chip made me another outfit, a fully beaded outfit. From that time on, I remained a Fancy Shawl dancer. I was placing at all the pow-wows in this area. I was placing about third, then I got to a point where I was placing first all the time, when I was probably fourteen, fifteen, sixteen. And what really helped me with dancing was being involved with sports in high school. I mean, I was active in all the sports in high school, basketball, softball, volleyball, so that really conditioned me for the weekends and for the summer. And to keep dancing, 'cause you do have to have a lot of stamina when you dance Fancy Shawl dancing.

Right around when I was sixteen or seventeen, I went jumping into the adult women's category, and I would have to compete against Punkin. So Punkin and I were going head to head when I was sixteen and seventeen years old—my older sister and the one who taught me to dance and outfitted me. So I always felt bad when I would beat her.

Still being the baby, I never had to braid my hair or learn how to braid my hair. My sisters would get ready, or while they were getting ready, I'd say, "Punkin, you've got to braid my hair." You can still hear me doing that, and I'm twenty-seven years old. So, being the baby you get pampered. I can make it on my own without them, but when they're around, I'll ask them to still braid my hair for me at pow-wow.

Just recently I've turned Traditional—I think it was three years ago. I've been an avid skier since high school. And three years ago I got into quite a tumble on Sugarloaf Mountain in Traverse City. And I tore my A-C ligament, my anterior cruciate ligament in my knee. I've lost all stability in my left knee. So therefore I can't Jingle, and I can't Fancy Shawl dance. I've since then turned Traditional, which I've really come to enjoy. And learned—watching my mother all these years has really helped me to dance Traditional. A lot of people think there's not too much to it, being a woman's Traditional dancer. It's lower [in footwork height], yet you have to have a carriage about you and that respect and that dignified manner and know the story and the teachings that go behind being a Traditional woman's dancer. Your feet never totally leave the ground because of that connection with Mother Earth. That connection we have as women to our Mother the Earth, and that dancing with those teachings, and that knowledge has really given me a lot of strength—being a woman's Traditional dancer.

Tara: Do you dance with your mom then?

Shannon: Yes. I dance with my mom now [laughs]. But I've thought about one day maybe having surgery to restructure my knee.

Tara: My mom had that, it's awful.

Shannon: Yeah, I hear it's awful.

Tara: She had a torn A-C ligament that was really bad, and her leg was in a huge cast.

Shannon: I hear it's pretty awful, they have to take ligament from somewhere else and place it in your knee.

Tara: Dead person's ligament.

Shannon: Yeah.

Tara: That's what they did with her.

Shannon: And you have to regrow it, and you have to have six months, maybe more, on a brace and then another year in rehab.

Tara: Um-hum.

Shannon: But I've thought about it on and off. I do miss Shawl dancing, and maybe I could be a Jingle Dress dancer. But I have come to enjoy being a Traditional woman dancer, and that has kind of put those thoughts out of my head. But regardless, I would still—not the pow-wow, not the dancing—I would still like to ski again. I do miss skiing [laughs]! And that would be something to think about. But I'm twenty seven and I've got to do surgery soon, to bounce back, I don't want to wait till I'm in my forties or something [laughs]. That would be horrible.

All those years with the drum and dancing have given our family a lot of strength. And just the whole community of the pow-wow: People looking out for each other and adults that have looked after me when I was a child running around. And now, becoming part of the circle it comes around, and now it's me looking after other people's children and making sure they're out there dancing or their outfit's tied up right and that they're not getting into trouble and giving them a dollar to go get a snow-cone or something. Now it's me who's in that role of watching over the children and making sure things are okay. So that pow-wow, it's really something. And it's the drum that holds it all together: The heartbeat of our people. Without it, we wouldn't have a whole lot. Because that drum is our center, and it always will be.

Tara: Your dad actually did a diagram for me of the seven circles coming out. And labeled them and everything.

Shannon: They say that first sound of the creation was that shaker that you hear, which accompanies the drum in a lot of ceremonies. And then after the shaker there was silence. And then came the heartbeat of the people and of life coming. That's what the drum is, that heartbeat.

Tara: I heard Eddie Benton tell a story, and in it he has two shakers, he has a copper shaker and a gourd shaker. And he said that you need these sounds. So first there was the sound of the shaker—is this a story from the Midewiwin?

Shannon: Um-hum.

Tara: Okay. Is that something you can talk about?

Shannon: I can, yeah, I can tell a little bit. But that's the sound of creation, first creation is the shaker. The sound of things spinning, of spinning and being put together.

Tara: Okay.

Shannon: Yeah, that's how I know it. And then comes the heartbeat after that. That signifies the life, not only of people but of everything that has life. The trees, the flowers, the water. It all has life and it's that *boom boom—boom boom—boom boom,* that's all part of it.

When I was talking earlier about myself even dancing before I was born, I probably was, in my mother's womb. And then coming into this world, being next to the drum in my cradleboard. That's why to this day you can always see babies sleeping right next to drums. There's no problem with it. That's just our people. You'll see other walks of life, other colors of people, children will be holding their ears because it's too loud, and other people holding their ears, thinking, gosh it's too loud, and then you'll walk by and see babies nestled right in with their families right by the drum and sleeping as peacefully as can be. And that's because they know instinctively that sound. So they come to recognize it when they start putting their little moccasin tracks on the earth and dancing. That's all part of it, that cycle.

Tara: Let's talk about when you're dancing and you hear the music. A lot of people talk about the drum, and then they talk about the words and the melodies and things like that. When you're dancing, do you do things with your footwork, for example, or how do you react to different songs and things like that?

Shannon: When I was Fancy Shawl dancing, I heard some of the songs and got to know a lot of the songs at pow-wows. But still, there're always times when you're dancing that you haven't heard a song before. And you can usually pick up the first verse and then know how that song is going to be, because the first verse is always repeated. You hear the lead singer's voice, then the rest of the singers join in, and then the beat. You can tell by the beat of the drum and the harder strikes on the drum that it's going to speed up. Then you can tell by the honor beats how much longer the song is going to last. So when you're dancing, it's not like *A Chorus Line* or something, where you have everything rehearsed, and you go into the song thinking, okay, this is the third honor beat, here's where I go into my four-spinning-ticking footwork.

Tara: That makes me think of those Olympic ice skaters.

Shannon: Yeah, where they can stand there and hear the music and picture their whole routine in their mind. That's not how we are. What we see, we dance. We dance for the music the way it is playing presently. I've never had a routine when I'm dancing. It's just how I feel. The steps I do and the spins I make and the moves and the directions I go in are how I feel with that song at that time. It's not some made-up routine, and I don't practice to one song for six months and then break out in summertime and have a whole choreographed routine. It's the feeling that you have at that time with that drum. That's that connection and that's how you express yourself for the drum and for the Creator.

Tara: That's good. I haven't gotten anybody else to quite lay it out like that, with that kind of connection.

Shannon: But I can't speak for some of the men Traditional dancers. Some of them do tell their stories to certain songs. For some of the songs—traditional songs—they will tell their story. And I don't really think that's choreographed. They'll tell their story in their own way when they're dancing. And that goes for any song, whether it be intertribal, a contest song, Crow Hop, or Sneak-up. It's your connection at that time, in the present, that is how you feel and how you dance.

Tara: Is there anything that you think is important that should be said or be in the book or anything else?

[Shannon laughs.]

Tara: I said that to your dad, and he said something that's really quotable!

Shannon: Oh, did he?

Tara: Yeah, he went into the teachings about respect for the Creation, and that was great! But you don't have to if you don't want to—if you're not feeling that eloquent.

Shannon: Um—well I just think that we really have to maintain these teachings and this way of life. It gives us all our strength. And we were always orators, where we would sit and talk verbally and vocally and pass on our teachings. But as time goes on, we've always adapted as people, and that's what's kept us going. You know, we've learned to adapt to the changing times. So I feel that's what you're doing with this book. This is something that is well needed, that we need to continue on this tradition. Hopefully, my great-great-great granddaughter or grandson will see this book. And that's a legacy that we leave for those ones that aren't here. To learn these things and put them down in a way that they can always hear it and remember it. So, *miigwetch.*

Tara: Thank you

———————

On September 1, 2000, Shannon Martin was suspended without pay from her position at the University of Michigan. Initially she was given no reason other than vague allegations of financial misconduct, and within a few days of the suspension the Ann Arbor police appeared at her apartment with a search warrant that had been sought by the university. After rummaging through Shannon's belongings and those of her roommate Gina, the police confiscated four Pendleton blankets, including Shannon's grandmother's funeral blanket and another that had been gifted to her during a Midewiwin Lodge ceremony. As part of the suspension, she was forbidden to set foot upon University of Michigan property.

At the December hearing on her suspension, the university set forth ninety-one allegations of financial misconduct, most having to do with the improper use of a university-owned vehicle and occurring during the spring and summer of 2000. It was on those trips—which the university counsel claimed were vacations—that Shannon repatriated the Indian objects taken from the Michigamua clubhouse during the Students of Color takeover, returning them to various tribal communities. Other charges included using university funds to purchase four Pendleton blankets for personal use, although Shannon's supervisors had been present when the blankets in question were presented to guest speakers. The investigation of Shannon's office financial records was instigated by the office of Dean of Students Frank Cianciola, the faculty advisor for Michigamua. Calls to his office went unanswered, and Vice President for Student Affairs Royster Harper has told me that she was "unable to comment because this is a personnel matter." As of the winter of 2000 Shannon was still under suspension, although she had retained an attorney to fight the charges.

Afterword: When the
Pow-wow's Over, Sweetheart . . .

With pow-wow performance existing for most of its participants and audience as a contemporary form with a historical past, what
is the genre's future? A number of possibilities present themselves based
upon recent trends and innovative new venues for performance. Most
immediately, with the ongoing (and seemingly unstoppable) revenue
growth being experienced by Indian casinos, more and more pow-wows
will be offering major prize money—at least $1,500 for the winners in
every category. That factor alone means that the caste of professional
competition dancers will expand, and the contest season, generally mid-
March through late October, also will lengthen with added indoor events.

Other than competitive extravaganzas, are there any other venues for
pow-wow style singing and dancing? Two different performance models
that are currently touring the United States, Canada, and Europe suggest
a future for Indian dancing outside the traditional and competition are-
nas. The American Indian Dance Theater and a touring musical, *Spirit:
A Journey of Dance, Drums, and Song*, both use pow-wow music and
dance forms but in radically different ways.

The American Indian Dance Theater was founded in 1987 by Hanay
Geiogamah (Kiowa/Delaware) and Barbara Schwei. Both were based in
New York, with Geiogamah a prominent playwright and theater director and Schwei a concert and theatrical producer. Together they created
the concept of a dance theater based upon traditional and contemporary
indigenous performance styles and set to work recruiting dancers and

musicians from an obvious source: pow-wows. Traveling the competition circuit, they carefully choose dancers and musicians who, in addition to having ability, possessed, they felt, a charisma that carried beyond the stage. Then Geiogamah conceptualized and created a series of dance "suites" based on traditional forms (primarily pow-wow dances but including tribal-specific styles), set them to music, and taught them to the dancers. The first tour was amazingly successful, and the company—which is not full time—has re-formed every two to three years since for a new tour that has included Europe, the Middle East, and Australia.

Spirit: A Journey of Dance, Drums, and Song had an entirely different genesis than the American Indian Dance Theater although it seems to share the same audience. Created in 1998 by Peter Buffet, who designed the musical score for *Dances with Woves,* and Hawk Pope, a musician, artist, and a member of Ohio's United Remnant Band of Shawnee (a tribe recognized by the state but not the federal government), *Spirit* has a sensibility distinct from the Dance Theater's performances. The most immediate difference between the two is *Spirit*'s use of a mixture of Native and non-Native dance styles, electric and acoustic instrumentation, and a narrative text in English and Anishnaabeg. The Native-language narration, done by Hawk Pope, was in a language that sounded very much like Eastern Ojibwe, although perhaps Shawnee and Ojibwe share certain similarities.

The premise of *Spirit* is that a young man, living in the mechanized modern world, gradually finds his Indian "hidden heritage." The show is a visually and musically exciting collage of sound and dance, at times almost overwhelming, with musicians foregrounded and sharing the dancer's stage. All of the Native musicians (particularly Robert Mirabal playing flute, eagle-bone whistle, and other wind instruments) are in various forms of Indian traditional dress and perform theatrically as well as musically. Native dancers dress in full pow-wow regalia, and non-Native dancers, including the one with "hidden heritage," are outfitted in various forms of Western business or modern dancewear (tank tops and black or gray leotards or capri pants). The dancing seems intended to contrast sterile, modern (or postmodern) regimentation with older, indigenous ways of personal freedom and relationships to the earth—in other words, the old "noble savage" trope with a New Age musical twist. Although well intended, the overall textual narrative of *Spirit* incorporates far too many New Age aspects, and although it showcases pow-wow dancing it does nothing particularly new with it.

In contrast, Geiogamah and Schwei's Dance Theater productions excel at innovation. In January 2001, Geiogamah invited me to the Dance

Theater's final rehearsal in Hollywood before it embarked upon its 2001 tour. The production, he told me before the rehearsal, would look very different than an actual performance because dancers would not be wearing regalia. He was correct. It was startling. Seeing the different pow-wow styles without the motions of regalia made evident the highly rhythmic and virtuosic nature of these dances. Most amazing was that Geiogamah, who teaches in the Department of Theater at UCLA, had taught the show to the dancers in three days, including new, modern-dance-style moves that some company members had never experienced. Blanca Jensen, the tour manager, told me after of the rehearsal of the speed with which dancers had picked up the new moves. "Talent is talent," I replied. "Period."

Aside from the music, glitz, and verbiage about "tradition," the primary difference between the American Indian Dance Theater's productions and *Spirit* lies in Geiogamah's vision of what pow-wow dancing is and what it could be. As Jennifer Fisher noted in a review that appeared in the *Los Angeles Times* on February 1, 2001, "Something wonderfully thought-provoking happened near the end of the latest American Indian Dance Theater program—it got minimalist. After an evening of sumptuously costumed traditional dance, with contemporary edges glimpsed here and there, 'Modern Fancy Dance' came along—six young dancers in black T-shirts and shorts, dancing without an overlay of symbols, stories or decorative adornment." Geiogamah, in many ways a traditionalist musically and aesthetically, understands that even in pre-contact Native societies, music and dance never stood still. They always changed and incorporated elements from the outside without sacrificing what he takes as the dance's "basic integrity and meaning." In essence the concept of change is itself a tradition.

NOTES

1. All about Theory, Method, and Pow-wows

1. My source of information on the American Mountain Man Society is my cousin Tom Sisco, an avid participant in the society for decades. According to Tom, any item that did not exist, or was not used as trade goods, before 1840 is prohibited at rendezvous. That does not mean that all gear is antique, but rather that it must be an honest facsimile. For example, smaller, "seed" beads are not allowed on clothing because they were not traded to tribes until the late 1850s. Only pony beads (larger than size 10) can be used.

2. "Northern" and "Southern," as ways to describe pow-wows, are Indian terms derived from geographic areas and not related to culture-area theory.

3. As influential as his theories were, it is important to keep in mind that Morgan was, by trade, the 1800s' version of a real estate agent.

4. Taking that fact into account, Judith Vander's *Songprints: The Musical Experience of Five Shoshone Women* (1988) contains the most comprehensive description of Northern pow-wow music available as well as a dense collection of transcriptions spread throughout the chapters on Helen Furlong (119–93) and Lenore Shoyo (195–284). Thomas Vennum's *Ojibway Music from Minnesota: A Century of Song for Voice and Drum* (1989), a fifteen-page booklet accompanying a cassette tape, includes a brief (six-page) section entitled "The Anatomy of a Powwow: Bemidji." It contains musical analysis, comparisons of singing style, and some historical background, although its length precludes greater depth. Although it does not focus on pow-wows, Vennum's *The Ojibwe Dance Drum: Its History and Construction* (1982) provides a good overview of Great Lakes and Northern Plains war dance styles before 1900. In his "In the Tradition: Grass Dance Musical Style and Female Pow-wow Singers" (1986), Orin Hatton deals primarily with Ojibwe musicians and analyzes some pow-wow repertory. In *Blackfoot Musical Thought: Comparative Perspectives* (1989), although he is primarily concerned with a tribal-specific traditional musical repertory, Bruno Nettl also includes a brief discussion of the major Blackfoot pow-wow, North American Indian Days. In his valuable *War Dance: Plains Indian Musical Performance* (1990), William Powers discusses vocable origins and Lakota singing styles. In spite of its broad title, however, the book is Lakota-centric. Gertrude Kurath's *Michigan Indian Festivals* (1966), the best overview of Great Lakes–area pow-wows during the 1950s and 1960s, includes photographs and transcriptions. Severt Young Bear and R. D. Theisz's *Standing in the Light: A Lakota Way of Seeing* (1994), although a wonderful telling of the life of a Lakota singer, lacks formalistic mu-

sical analysis. Thus, other than James Howard's work, the only major scholarly treatment to include a broad discussion of Southern pow-wow music at present is Lassiter's *The Power of Kiowa Song: A Collaborative Ethnography* (1998).

5. The most far-reaching document related to contemporary pow-wow life is Gloria Young's 1981 dissertation: "Powwow Power: Perspectives on Historic and Contemporary Intertribalism." Young's study is an ethnography of the Tulsa Pow-wow, a Southern-style event, and although she includes valuable historic background on pow-wow origins (primarily Southern), Young does not discuss music in any detail. George Horse Capture's *Powwow* (1989), the catalog from a museum exhibit, focuses primarily on historical origins of dance regalia and specific dances. *Native American Dance: Ceremonies and Social Traditions* (Heth, ed. 1992) includes a chapter by Lynn Huenemann on Northern pow-wows, but as a general overview it provides only limited coverage of musical repertories. Anthropologist Joan Weibel-Orlando's *Indian Country L.A.: Maintaining Ethnic Community in Complex Society* (1991) deals with issues of identity at urban pow-wows, but primarily in the Southern tradition.

Chapter 2: People and Histories

1. For example, the Sisseton-Wahpeton Sioux (South Dakota) referred to their year 2000 "Millennium Wacipi" as the 133d annual event, which would date their first as being in 1867. The Nebraska Winnebago do one year better, giving the year 1866 as the first in which they held their homecoming celebration in honor of Chief Little Priest. The White Earth Pow-wow in Minnesota claims a starting date of 1878. In Oklahoma, the Ponca give the first year of their pow-wow as 1884, but then qualify their claim to the oldest pow-wow by saying that theirs was the first in Oklahoma. The oldest published claim in a pow-wow advertisement that I have seen was that of the 196th Annual Harvest Celebration in Macy, Nebraska, by the Omaha Tribe. None of these events seem to have been intertribal in their earliest years, and whether or not they have been held continuously is open to question. Probably the longest-running *intertribal* pow-wow is Crow Fair at the Crow Agency in Montana, which began in 1918.

2. William Powers, who apart from Ronnie Theisz is one of the foremost non-Indian experts on Lakota and Northern Great Plains music, stated (1963) that the modern pow-wow version of Grass dancing is the same as the old Omaha/Grass Dance. To be fair, he does so in an article intended for hobbyists (non-Indian pow-wow dancers). Even in 1963, however, Powers had been dancing and studying Lakota music for more than a decade.

3. In 1840 the Pawnee were living in the mid-Prairie and Plains areas of eastern Nebraska in immediate proximity to the Omaha/Ponca people, who at that time were a single tribal unit.

4. By "Americans," I mean specifically those who had citizenship. American Indians were not granted American citizenship until 1924.

5. Because Powers considers Omaha and Grass dancing to be identical, this statement is also incorrect. Numerous recordings of Lakota Grass Dance songs of the 1950s and 1960s include Lakota yelps. One example is Ben Black Bear and his family's performance on *Songs of the Sioux* (Canyon Records 6062), which was made in the late 1950s.

6. The collected field recordings and field notes of Willard Rhodes are housed in the ethnomusicology archive at the University of California, Los Angeles. Because they are only partially cataloged, it is not possible to provide a complete reference for this song other than Rhodes Collection, volume 2.

7. The right to use ("carry") pipes—specifically those made of "pipestone" (catlinite)—is a matter of ongoing contention in Indian Country. Many Lakota claim that the White Buffalo Calf Pipe is *the* original pipe, and all other pipes draw legitimacy from it. Using that claim of ownership, individual Lakota people have been known to question publicly the use of pipes by non-Lakota, even if the pipes are not made of pipestone. When I worked at the Smithsonian Folklife Festival in Washington, D.C., during July 1996, for example, a Catabwa artist was in residence, making traditional Catabwa molded-clay pipes. One afternoon a Lakota man appeared and challenged the Catabwa artist's "right" to make pipes, citing the White Buffalo Calf Woman story. I intervened in the argument (as part of my job), and in the ensuing discussion it became clear that the Lakota man did not recognize the legitimacy of pipe traditions outside his own, even when they predated the White Buffalo Calf Pipe.

8. A dry dance is an alcohol-free, post–pow-wow gathering where music is provided by both Drum groups and hand drum–playing singers.

9. Nadine Rendon was the mother of Norma Rendon, the consultant whose family is featured in chapter 5.

Chapter 3: Dance Styles and Regalia

1. The following are excerpts from my letter of July 6, 1994, to Allan Crow. My collaborator for the project is identified as X for purposes of privacy.

This letter is in reference to our conversation of about two weeks ago, when we discussed your Jingle Dress Dance research, and a paper on Jingle Dancing that I am currently co-writing with a colleague at the University of Michigan, X. . . .

The article we are working on is concerned with the origins of the Jingle Dress dance, and how the origin story has changed to fit the needs of each People who have taken up the dance, but the heart of the story has remained the same. The article could also include regional variations in dance style and regalia, as well as differing perceptions of the meaning of the dance and its importance. . . .

X and I would welcome your contribution to this project, either as a collaborator or as a co-author, whatever your preference. X will be taking photographs for the article at the Grand River Champion of Champions Pow-wow at Six Nations the third week of July. If you are at that pow-wow you could meet with him there. Many of the people in charge there know him, and would be able to point him out to you. . . .

I will be in Minneapolis the last weekend of October to give a paper, perhaps we could meet there if you are on your way through to Chicago Pow-wow. I also plan on attending the Minneapolis Pow-wow this fall, which I understand to be the third weekend in November. . . .

One way or the other, I hope this proposal interests you, and look forward to your participation.

Chapter 4: Making and Singing Songs

1. The Wisconsin and Nebraska Winnebago are the major exception to the concept of Northern and Southern singing and pow-wow styles being purely geographical. The Winnebago (now called the Ho-Chunk in Wisconsin) sing in a Southern manner but dance in the Northern style, notably substituting men's Northern Traditional dancing for the men's Southern Straight and the more static women's Buckskin category for Southern Cloth dancing.

2. Hatton's article is on the Grass Dance, a Northern style, and his historic periods correspond with changes happening in those repertoires as well as extra-musical changes in dance styles.

3. For the specific dates of Rhodes's recordings, see Korson and Hickerson (1969:296–304).

4. In Northern pow-wow terminology, "Traditional" or "Word" songs are those which include Native language texts, whereas "Straight" song texts are composed of vocables only.

5. The 1990 citation is a revised reprint originally published in 1970 as "Songs of the Red Man: New Releases from American Indian Soundchiefs," *Ethnomusicology* 14(2):358–69.

6. "Omaha" and "Grass Dance" are the Northern versions; "O'ho-ma" is the Southern Comanche/Kiowa name for the warrior society and its dance.

7. Occasionally, a song without an interior repetition of the strophe can be heard, most often in the Northern Crow Hop category.

Chapter 5: Pow-wows in Space and Time

1. Problems usually arise when point systems are simplistic, for example 50 points for third, 100 points for second, and 150 points for first. At one pow-wow I attended, every category required a dance-off for that reason. Norma Rendon, who was with me, was asked to judge at that event. She later told me that the Oglala Nation pow-wow, where she often judges, uses an even-odd point system—for example, 51 (third), 102 (second), and 153 (first)—and avoids ties.

2. The largest pow-wows last from Thursday through Sunday, with the first grand entry at 1 P.M. on Thursday. Dances that begin on Fridays usually have their first grand entry at 7 P.M., with the Friday session reserved for intertribals, exhibitions, and specials.

3. Head Drums are those invited to a pow-wow and paid for their performance. Other Drums can also be invited and paid, and still more Drums show up (unless a pow-wow is designated as for invited Drums only) and play for day money gathered through a Blanket Dance. The purpose of appointing some Drums as head Drums is that it guarantees a level of musical competence and attracts dancers.

4. Credit for the term *pow-wow potato* belongs to Kelly Jasinski (Seneca) and Shawna Red Cloud (Lakota).

BIBLIOGRAPHY

Anacona, George. 1993. *Powwow*. San Diego: Harcourt Brace.

Andrist, Ralph K. 1964. *The Long Death: The Last Days of the Plains Indians*. New York: Collier Books.

Arias, Annie. 1999. "Weekend World Is Full-Time." *News from Indian Country* 18(8): 22.

Around Him, John, and Albert White Hat. 1983. *Lakota Ceremonial Songs*. Rosebud, S.D.: Sinte Gleska College.

Ashworth, Kenneth Albert. 1986. "The Contemporary Oklahoma Pow-wow." Ph.D. diss. University Oklahoma.

Axtmann, Ann. 1999. "Dance: Celebration and Resistance, Native American Indian Intertribal Powwow Performance." Ph.D. diss. New York University.

Bakan, Michael B. 1999. *Music of Death and New Creation: Experiences in the World of Balinese Gamelan Beleganjur*. Chicago: University of Chicago Press.

Bennett, Helen Marie. 1902. "The Indian Dances." *Southern Workman* 31(6): 345–48.

Black Bear, Ben, Sr., and R. D. Theisz. 1976. *Songs and Dances of the Lakota*. Aberdeen, S.D.: North Plains Press.

Brown, Vanessa, and Barre Toelken. 1987. "American Indian Powwow." *Folklife Annual* 46–69.

Browner, Tara. 1995. "A Reexamination of the *Peji Waci*." *American Music Center Research Journal* 5: 71–81.

———. 2000. "Making and Singing Pow-wow Songs: Text, Form, and the Significance of Culture-Based Analysis." *Ethnomusicology* 44(2): 214–33.

Burke, Charles. 1921. *Indian Dancing*. Circular 1665. Washington, D.C.: Office of Indian Affairs.

———. 1923. *Indian Dancing*. Supplement to Circular 1665. Washington, D.C.: Office of Indian Affairs.

Clifford, James. 1988. *The Predicament of Culture: Twentieth-Century Ethnography, Literature, and Art*. Cambridge: Harvard University Press.

Clifton, James A. 1986 "Potawatomi." In *People of the Three Fires: The Ottawa, Potawatomi, and Ojibway of Michigan*, ed. James A. Clifton, George L. Cornell, and James M. McClurken, 39–74. Grand Rapids: Michigan Indian Press, Grand Rapids Inter-Tribal Council.

Compisi, Jack. 1975. "Powwow: A Study of Ethnic Boundary Maintenance." *Man in the Northeast* 9: 34–46.

Cornell, George L. 1986. "Ojibway." In *People of the Three Fires: The Ottawa, Potawatomi, and Ojibway of Michigan*, ed. James A. Clifton, George L. Cornell, and James M. McClurken, 75–108. Grand Rapids: Michigan Indian Press, Grand Rapids Inter-Tribal Council.

Corrigan, Samuel W. 1970. "The Plains Indian Powwow: Cultural Integration in Manitoba Saskatchewan." *Anthrologica* 12(2): 253–77.

Crow, Allan. 1994. Personal communication, Aug. 9.

Dashner, Michael. 1989. Ann Arbor Pow-wow program.

Densmore, Frances. 1910. *Chippewa Music.* Bureau of American Ethnology Bulletin 45. Washington D.C.: Government Printing Office.

———. 1913. *Chippewa Music II.* Bureau of American Ethnology Bulletin 53. Washington D.C.: Government Printing Office.

———. 1915. "The Study of Indian Music." *Musical Quarterly* 1(1): 187–97.

———. 1918. *Teton Sioux Music.* Bureau of American Ethnology Bulletin 61. Washington D.C.: Government Printing Office.

———. 1929. *Pawnee Music.* Bureau of American Ethnology Bulletin 93. Washington D.C.: Government Printing Office.

———, ed. 1951a. *Songs of the Pawnee and Northern Ute.* Folk Music of the United States series. AAFS L25. Washington D.C.: Library of Congress, Division of Music, Recording Laboratory.

———, ed. 1951b. *Songs of the Sioux.* Folk Music of the United States series. AAFS L23. Washington D.C.: Library of Congress, Division of Music, Recording Laboratory.

Diamond, Beverly, with M. Sam Cronk and Franziska von Rosen. 1994. *Visions of Sound: Musical Instruments of First Nations Communities in Northeastern America.* Chicago: University of Chicago Press.

Drum, Jacob, with Lawrence Gilpin, Rudolph Clark, and John Turner. 1972. *Omaha Singers.* Fay, Okla.: Indian Records.

Dyck, Noel. 1979. "Powwow and the Expression of Community in Western Canada." *Ethos* 44: 78–90.

———. 1983. "Political Powwow: The Rise and Fall of an Urban Native Festival." In *The Celebration of Society: Perspectives on Contemporary Cultural Performance,* ed. Frank E. Manning, 165–84. Bowling Green: Bowling Green University Popular Press.

Edmunds, R. David. 1978. *The Potawatomies: Keepers of the Fire.* Norman: University of Oklahoma Press.

Feyerabend, Paul. 1993. *Against Method.* New York: Verso Press.

Fisher, Jennifer. 2001."They're Developing New Traditions." *Los Angeles Times,* Feb. 1, 58.

Fitting, James E. 1975. *The Archeology of Michigan.* Bloomfield Hills, Mich.: Cranfield Institute of Science.

Fletcher, Alice Cunningham. 1893. *A Study of Omaha Indian Music.* Cambridge: Peabody Museum of American Archeology and Ethnology.

———. 1900. *Indian Story and Song from North America.* Boston: Small, Maynard.

Gilbert, Tamara B. 1991. "Urban Powwows: Form and Meaning." *UCLA Journal of Dance Ethnology* 15: 78–90.

Goertzen, Chris. 2001. "Powwows and Identity on the Piedmont and Coastal Plains of North Carolina." *Ethnomusicology* 45(1): 58–88.

Hatton, Orin. 1974. "Performance Traditions of Northern Plains Pow-wow Singing Groups." *Yearbook for Inter-American Musical Research* 10: 123–37.

———. 1986. "In the Tradition: Grass Dance Musical Style and Female Pow-wow Singers." *Ethnomusicology* 30(2): 197–219

———. 1988. "'We Caused Them to Cry': Power and Performance in Gros Ventres War Expedition Songs." Master's thesis, Catholic University of America.

Heth, Charlotte, ed. 1992. *Native American Dance: Ceremonies and Social Traditions.* Washington, D.C.: Smithsonian Instution Press.

Horse Capture, George P. 1989. *Powwow.* Cody, Wyo.: Buffalo Bill Historical Center.

Howard, James. 1983. "Pan-Indianism in Native American Music and Dance." *Ethnomusicology* 28(1): 71–82.

Isaacs, Tony. 1959. "Oklahoma Singing." *American Indian Hobbyist* 5(9): 106–10.

Jones, Judith Ann. 1995. "'Women Never Used to War Dance': Gender and Music in Nez Perce Culture Change." Ph.D. diss., Washington State University.

Kelly, Lawrence C. 1983. *The Assault on Assimilation: John Collier and the Origins of Indian Policy Reform.* Albuquerque: University of New Mexico Press.

Korson, Rae, and Joseph C. Hickerson. 1969. "The Willard Rhodes Collection of American Indian Music in the Archive of Folk Song." *Ethnomusicology* 13(2): 296–305.

Kracht, Benjamin R. 1994. "Kiowa Powwows: Continuity in Ritual Practice." *American Indian Quarterly* 18(3): 321–48.

Krouse, Susan Applegate. 1991. "A Window into the Indian Culture: The Powwow as Performance." Ph.D. diss., University of Wisconsin, Milwaukee.

Kurath, Gertrude Prokosch. 1966. *Michigan Indian Festivals.* Ann Arbor: Ann Arbor Publishers.

Lassiter, Luke E. 1998. *The Power of Kiowa Song: A Collaborative Ethnography.* Tucson: University of Arizona Press.

Laudin, Harvey Golden. 1973. "The Shinnecock Powwow: A Study of Culture Change." Ed.D. diss., New York University.

McClurken, James M. 1986. "Ottawa." In *People of the Three Fires: The Ottawa, Potawatomi, and Ojibway of Michigan,* ed. James A. Clifton, George L. Cornell, and James M. McClurken, 1–38. Grand Rapids: Michigan Indian Press, Grand Rapids Inter-Tribal Council.

McCracken, Harold. 1959. *George Catlin and the Old Frontier.* New York: Dial Press.

Mendoza, Zoila S. 2000. *Shaping Society through Dance: Mestizo Ritual Performance in the Peruvian Andes.* Chicago: University of Chicago Press.

Mitchell-Green, Bonnie Lynn. 1995. "American Indian Powwows in Utah, 1983–1994: A Case Study in Oppositional Culture." Ph.D. diss., University of Texas at Austin.

Murie, James R. 1914. "Pawnee Indian Societies." *Anthropological Papers of the American Museum of Natural History* 11(7): 545–644.

Nettl, Bruno. 1954. *North American Indian Musical Styles.* Philadelphia: American Folklore Society.

———. 1989. *Blackfoot Musical Thought: Comparative Perspectives.* Kent: Kent State University Press.

Ortiz, Simon. 1977. *Song, Poetry, and Language—Expression and Perception.* Tsaile, Ariz.: Navajo Community College Press.

Peterson, Julie. 2000. "Three Student Groups to Be Relocated." *University* [of Michigan] *Record*, Aug. 14.

Philip, Kenneth R. 1977. *John Collier's Crusade for Indian Reform, 1920–1954*. Tucson: University of Arizona Press.

Powers, William K. 1963. *Grass Dance Costume*. Somerset, N.J.: Pow-wow Trails.

———. 1966. *Here Is Your Hobby: Indian Dancing and Costumes*. New York: G. P. Putnam's Sons.

———. 1980. "Oglala Song Terminology." In *Selected Reports on Ethnomusicology*, ed. Charlotte Heth. Los Angeles: Program in Ethnomusicology, University of California, Los Angeles.

———. 1987. *Beyond the Vision: Essays on American Indian Culture*. Norman: University of Oklahoma Press.

———. 1990. *War Dance: Plains Indian Musical Performance*. Tucson: University of Arizona Press.

Pratt, Mary Louise. 1986. "Fieldwork in Common Places." In *Writing Culture: The Poetics and Politics of Ethnography*, ed. James Clifford and George E. Marcus, 27–50. Berkeley: University of California Press.

Rhodes, Willard, ed. 1954a. *Kiowa*. Folk Music of the United States series. AFS L35. Washington D.C.: Library of Congress, Music Division, Recording Laboratory.

———. 1954b. *Plains: Comanche, Cheyenne, Kiowa, Caddo, Wichita, Pawnee*. AFS L39. Washington D.C.: Library of Congress, Music Division, Recording Laboratory.

———. 1954c. *Sioux*. Music of the American Indian series. AFS L40. Washington D.C.: Library of Congress, Music Division, Recording Laboratory.

Riggs, Stephen. 1894. *Dakota Grammer, Texts, and Ethnography*. Vol. 9. Washington: Contributions to North American Ethnology.

Roberts, Helen H. 1936. *Musical Areas in Aboriginal North America*. New Haven: Yale University Press for the Section on Anthropology, Department of Social Sciences.

Ronda, James R. 1984. *Lewis and Clark among the Indians*. Lincoln: University of Nebraska Press.

Rosaldo, Renato. 1989. *Culture and Truth: The Remaking of Social Analysis*. Boston: Beacon Press.

Sanchez, Victoria Eugenie. 1995. "'As Long as We Dance, We Shall Know Who We Are': A Study of Off-Reservation Traditional Intertribal Powwows in Central Ohio." Ph.D. diss., Ohio State University.

Seguine, Joel. 2000. "Panel Releases Recommendations for the Allocation of Space." *University* [of Michigan] *Record*, April 24.

Slotkin, Richard. 1993. "Buffalo Bill's 'Wild West' and the Mythologization of the American Empire." In *Cultures of United States Imperialism*, ed. Amy Kaplan and Donald E. Pease, 164–181. Durham, N.C.: Duke University Press.

Tivy, Mary. 1993. "Museums and Exhibits of First Nations: Old Paradigms and New Possibilities." *Ontario Museum Annual* 11: 6–18.

Young Bear, Severt, and R. D. Theisz. 1994. *Standing in the Light: A Lakota Way of Seeing*. Lincoln: University of Nebraska Press.

Young, Gloria Alese. 1981. "Powwow Power: Perspectives on Historic and Contemporary Intertribalism." Ph.D. diss., Department of Anthropology, Indiana University.

Vander, Judith. 1988. *Songprints: The Musical Experience of Five Shoshone Women.* Urbana: University of Illinois Press.

———. 1997. *Shoshone Ghost Dance Religion: Poetry Songs and Great Basin Context.* Urbana: University of Illinois Press.

Vennum, Thomas. 1980. "A History of Ojibwe Song Form." In *Selected Reports on Ethnomusicology,* ed. Charlotte Heth, 43–73. Los Angeles: Program in Ethnomusicology, University of California, Los Angeles.

———. 1982. *The Ojibwa Dance Drum: Its History and Construction.* Washington, D.C.: Smithsonian Institution Press.

———. 1989. *Ojibway Music from Minnesota: Continuity and Change.* St. Paul: Minnesota Historical Society Press.

Vogel, Virgil J. 1970. *American Indian Medicine.* Norman: University of Oklahoma Press.

Walker, James. 1980. *Lakota Ritual and Belief.* Edited by Raymond J. DeMallie and Elaine A. Jahner. Lincoln: University of Nebraska Press.

Weibel-Orlando, Joan. 1991. *Indian Country L.A.: Maintaining Ethnic Community in a Complex Society.* Urbana: University of Illinois Press.

Wissler, Clark. 1912. "Societies and Ceremonial Associations of the Oglala Division of the Teton-Dakota." *Anthropological Papers of the American Museum of Natural History* 11(1): 3–99.

———. 1916."General Discussion of Shamanistic and Dancing Societies." *Anthropological Papers of the American Museum of Natural History* 11(12): 853–76.

Whitehorse, David. 1988. *Pow-wow: The Contemporary Pan-Indian Celebration.* Publications in American Indian Studies 5. San Diego: San Diego State University.

Interviews

George and Sydney Martin, Sept. 16, 1996, Flint, Mich., and Sept. 17, 1997, Hopkins, Mich.

Shannon Martin, Sept. 18, 1997, Ann Arbor, Mich.

Norma Rendon, Aug. 15, 16, 1989, Boulder, Colo., and Aug. 22, 1997, Porcupine, S.D.

Robert Rendon, Aug. 22, 1997, Porcupine, S.D.

David and Punkin Shananaquet, Sept. 17, 1997, Hopkins, Mich.

INDEX

TARA BROWNER is an assistant professor of
ethnomusicology and American Indian studies at
the University of California, Los Angeles.

The University of Illinois Press
is a founding member of the
Association of American University Presses.

Composed in 9.5/12.5 Trump Mediaeval
with Trump Mediaeval display
by Jim Proefrock
at the University of Illinois Press
Manufactured by Thomson-Shore, Inc.

University of Illinois Press
1325 South Oak Street
Champaign, IL 61820-6903
www.press.uillinois.edu